*Whenever you share love with others, you'll
notice the peace that comes to you and to them.*

—MOTHER TERESA

# LOVE IS THE PATH

# LOVE IS THE PATH

AN IMMIGRANT'S JOURNEY TO
BELONGING THROUGH THE WORKPLACE

CLAUDIA CARDOZO

MANUSCRIPTS
**PRESS**

MANUSCRIPT PRESS



LOVE IS THE PATH

*An Immigrant's Journey to Belonging Through the Workplace*

ISBN  979-8-88926-113-1 *Paperback*
     979-8-88926-114-8 *Hardcover*
     979-8-88926-112-4 *Ebook*

# Contents

# Introduction

---

*When we are engaged in what
we are doing, we feel alive.*

—MIHALY CSIKSZENTMIHALYI

I secured a full-time job at the age of seventeen working at an apparel manufacturing company in Colombia to provide for my mom and younger sister. That job was the most significant accomplishment I had experienced at that point in my life. My job became a symbol of independence and freedom, liberating me from the group home where I lived for seven years alongside a few dozen girls my age, striving to follow the rules to avoid punishment. Despite my job requiring me to stand for several hours doing repetitive tasks, I was thrilled to have the financial means to support my family.

A similar experience occurred when I was rolling burritos and frying tacos at the age of twenty-five as a newly arrived immigrant in the United States, driven by a clear purpose to reunite with my daughter, which kept me motivated to work.

Over the years, I assimilated to the way of life in the United States and had the privilege of working in roles that tapped into my talents and passions, providing fulfillment. During the early years of my consumer banking career, I woke up eagerly every morning, ready to make a difference in people's lives. Teaching financial education and entrepreneurship gave me a sense of purpose, especially knowing I was helping young adults and mid- to low-income bracket families.

I experienced this great sense of purpose until my role evolved as a result of adapting to a post-COVID-19 era and regulatory adjustments affecting the industry. Due to the nature of these changes, I began feeling ill-prepared and inadequate to perform my best in my role. In those moments, I understood some of the disengaged employees I once judged back when my job and my purpose were one.

Gallup's 2023 *State of the Global Workplace* report revealed a global crisis of engagement, with only 23 percent of employees feeling engaged at work (2023). Many of these disengaged employees possess remarkable talents but struggle to align their strengths and passions with their work. Others may have never had the opportunity to truly enjoy their work and have settled for a job merely for the paycheck, devoid of any sense of job satisfaction.

In Gallup's book *Blind Spot: The Global Rise of Unhappiness and How Leaders Missed It*, Jon Clifton argues that while leaders track KPIs to measure progress, they are not systematically tracking how people feel, which is leading to a greater divide in "well-being inequality" (Clifton, 2022). Key metrics and measuring progress are crucial for a company's success, so why aren't all companies measuring employees' happiness? Stress and burnout not only affect the health of many individuals today but also impede organizations from harnessing the full potential of their people to be more resourceful and innovative.

I have gained a unique perspective on workplace cultures as an immigrant to the US and after years of prioritizing my career at the expense of my well-being. My experience assisting leaders in creating more inclusive environments has fueled my passion for advocating for compassionate leaders and conscious workplaces.

The year 2022 marked a period of deep self-reflection. I reevaluated the various facets of my life, especially how much I had disconnected from my cultural roots and my forgotten passion for dance. Was sacrificing parts of my heritage and striving to fit in over the past couple of decades worth it? How did I end up feeling so alone and unhappy? It felt as though my life was slipping away as I relentlessly pursued success and achievements rather than embracing my authentic self and fully experiencing life.

Later that year, following my departure from my corporate job, I embarked on a remarkable journey to Spain. That adventure was unlike any I had ever experienced before.

My prior travels had always been as a visitor, engaging in typical tourist activities, but this trip was different. I found myself in different places where I could interact with the locals and gain a deeper appreciation of Spanish values and culture. I found myself relishing every bite of the most delicious seafood tapas at a Basque restaurant in Barcelona. As I bit into a piece of toasted bread with soft white fish and delicate herbs garnishing the small delight, I savored the delicious sauces dripping through my fingers and became emotional, realizing I had never enjoyed food in this way.

While in Montserrat, a holy mountain range near Barcelona, I experienced an immense sense of peace and fulfillment for the first time in my life. As I sat by my hotel room window on a gorgeous fall afternoon, I felt immense gratitude for my life and the journey that had brought me to that very moment. I was overwhelmed by a sense of peace and joy and experienced a feeling of abundance for undertaking that trip for myself.

For most of my life, I felt I was lacking something. I was always running from one thing to the other, seeking to achieve something to feel good about myself. Seeking external validation and harshly judging myself and others became second nature, leading me down a path of unhappiness.

Society has conditioned us to believe love and validation come from the outside, but true, lasting love and validation only come from within. Through personal experiences, interviews, and research, I have come to understand relying on external validation makes us vulnerable and entangled in our egos. In doing so, we often suppress our true selves in pursuit of the approval we crave.

The concept of self-love is not new and dates back to the teachings of Buddhism. Reportedly, Buddha once said, "You yourself, as much as anybody in the entire universe, deserve your love and affection." More recently, researcher and thought leader Brené Brown, in her book *The Gifts of Imperfection: Let Go of Who You Think You're Supposed to Be and Embrace Who You Are*, asserts, "I now see how owning our story and loving ourselves through that process is the bravest thing that we will ever do" (Brown 2010, 11). Although we cognitively know the importance of self-love, the pressures of our society prevent many of us from fully embodying it. But only when we have that healthy relationship with ourselves can we have healthier relationships with others.

As I navigate my journey toward a more mindful and fulfilling life, I have come to realize many of us lack the essential skills required to genuinely connect with one another, comprehend our shared humanity, and honor each other's stories in a way that validates our distinct struggles and contributions.

Today, more than ever, we must collaborate to build bridges of understanding among one another. We must acknowledge that the only way we can thrive individually and collectively is by opening our hearts and connecting with the stories that make us human.

Join me as I delve introspectively into my life stories and the lessons I've learned from them. Together, let's cocreate a transformed workplace—a sanctuary for healing and personal growth.

## Mindfulness Moment

Mindfulness empowers us to embrace the present moment fully. It fosters a deep understanding of our emotions and the wisdom they hold. Take a moment to reflect on your professional journey and recall a moment when you truly loved what you were doing. Allow yourself to feel the joy and fulfillment this memory brings, acknowledging and appreciating your unique talents, passions, and strengths. As you breathe in, visualize love and acceptance entering your body, and as you breathe out, imagine releasing any self-judgment or negativity. The path to a more fulfilling life begins with self-love.

# PART I

# JOURNEY TO SELF

# CHAPTER 1

# My Immigrant Journey to Validation Within

---

*Giovanni: Love is a tremendous responsibility.*
*Baldwin: It's the only one to take,*
*there isn't any other.*

—JAMES BALDWIN AND NIKKI GIOVANNI,
*A DIALOGUE*

One Monday in the spring of 2018, gratitude overwhelmed me as I had the opportunity to speak to junior high school students at the MET school, a Metropolitan Regional Career and Technical Center breaking free from traditional education models and creating an environment that nurtures both the mind and the hearts of young people.

I experienced a great sense of purpose as I walked toward the front of the room, glancing at the motivational signs adorning the walls. The warmth and authenticity of the space filled me with joy to share my personal story.

I shared my immigrant journey with them, explaining the sacrifices I had to make in order to build a better future for me and my daughter. I recounted my experiences—from my first job rolling burritos and frying tacos at the food court in the Providence Place mall to the struggles of mastering a new language and navigating a foreign land alone. Many students, who either had immigrant backgrounds or were immigrants themselves, deeply connected with my story.

During that period, I held the position of community development manager at a local bank in Rhode Island. My primary responsibilities revolved around administering various aspects of the Community Reinvestment Act (CRA) compliance program. Additionally, I oversaw the employee volunteer program, managed the community donations budget, and spearheaded the financial education initiative.

Although managing the CRA compliance program was a new challenge for me, I excelled in my role. As the company expanded, I was entrusted with additional responsibilities, which allowed me to pursue what I am truly passionate about—actively engaging with the community and educating individuals and families on financial matters.

In the first three years at the bank, I successfully formed a team of ten committed financial educators, all of whom were esteemed colleagues from within the bank. Together, we conducted over one hundred financial education workshops in thirty-seven community organizations and schools, reaching out to a diverse group of over fifteen hundred participants. Each day, I had the privilege of making a positive impact on people's lives, and this sense of purpose resonated deeply within me.

Those years were the pinnacle of my career, as the experiences I had as an immigrant in the US became the foundation for supporting others on their path to integration and self-sufficiency.

I felt incredibly grateful to have a job that allowed me to serve, as giving back held profound meaning in my life. Every visit to the MET school was a remarkable journey. I experienced a profound bond with the students, and witnessing their eagerness for growth and learning left me with a sense of true fulfillment. The director of entrepreneurship, Jodie Woodruff, took their enthusiasm to new heights by encouraging students to express gratitude to guest speakers with handwritten letters. Receiving those heartfelt messages after my visits always brought me pure joy.

Here are a few of the handwritten letters from the youth:

*"Being from an immigrant family as well, I admire your drive to move forward. When you were telling your story about working in cleaning, it reminded me of my sister and her passion and drive to provide for our family."*

—LIANA, THE GIRL WITH THE PUFFY,<br>
CURLY HAIR IN THE FRONT

These letters were a precious gift to me. Whenever I spoke to the youth, I was prompted to reflect on my life, accomplishments, and the challenges I had overcome to reach that point in my career. Reading these letters indicated the life lessons I aimed to convey were being understood. The students were mirrors reflecting light and hope to me, giving me an extraordinary sense of purpose. I knew for some of them, coming home was challenging as they were not always supported, but I also knew they understood they had to believe in themselves to create the future they desired.

I felt the same joy and meaning in providing personalized financial coaching sessions to low-income women as part of my community engagement efforts. Those one-on-one interactions allowed me to connect with them in profound and intimate ways. I had the opportunity to learn about their dreams and aspirations and guide them in establishing goals and budgets that aligned with their values. Witnessing their "aha" moments when they realized they had the ability to choose and save money for things that matter most to them was truly rewarding.

For example, one of the women I coached was surprised to discover how much money she spent on fast food in a year. She said to me, "I do have money to take my family to a good restaurant; I just need to eat out less frequently." Others were able to save up for a reliable car or a down payment on a house.

## AN INVITATION TO LOOK WITHIN

In the autumn of 2018, the bank where I worked underwent an acquisition by a larger regional bank. While the announcement had been made earlier in the year, I didn't fully grasp the impact it would have on my role. Initially, the changes were subtle for me, as I had the privilege of being a member of an extraordinary team that shared the same dedication to serving the local population.

When the COVID-19 pandemic struck and forced us to stay indoors, I had to adjust my responsibilities and work approach accordingly. Instead of conducting in-person financial education classes and doing local volunteer work, I found myself delivering webinars and prerecorded classes for flexible viewing. In these virtual settings, I had limited interaction with participants and couldn't feel the impact I was making. I struggled to follow the webinar script, trying to imagine I was speaking to a client but feeling demotivated in the process. I wondered why other employees at the bank were having less difficulty adapting to these changes.

Apart from the impact of COVID-19, my responsibilities also changed due to revisions to the Community Reinvestment Act (CRA), a federal law that encourages financial institutions to meet the credit needs of the communities they serve, specifically low- and moderate-income neighborhoods. My primary role was aligned to serve these communities.

However, following the expansion of the bank's assessment area beyond Rhode Island and the implementation of new CRA mandates after the merger, our territory of service grew significantly. As a result, I could no longer engage in the grassroots work I had been deeply involved in within my local community or do personalized financial coaching sessions for individuals. I deeply missed the interactions with local organizations and the relationships I had fostered over the years in Rhode Island.

Although I was grateful to still have a job while some of my colleagues were let go, my dissatisfaction with my role grew steadily over the next couple of years. It became increasingly challenging to find fulfillment in my work. I decided to speak openly with my VP, expressing my discontent and my desire to pursue work that truly mattered to me. In an effort to reignite my passion, my VP presented the new company's incentive program, but unfortunately, it did not resonate with me. Monetary rewards were not my primary motivation. What drove me was the potential to make a positive impact on people's lives, touch their hearts, and inspire meaningful change.

In early 2022, I found myself feeling disengaged at work and overwhelmed with responsibilities that didn't align with my strengths. It left me feeling inadequate and questioning my ability to handle new assignments. The passion and drive I once had for my career had diminished. Upon reflection, I've come to realize the tasks themselves weren't inherently difficult. What made the tasks feel challenging was the misalignment with my values and sense of purpose. My situation worsened when I no longer had the autonomy to work on the community projects that gave me fulfillment. I later understood those interactions at work provided me with the human connection I needed.

Not only was I feeling demotivated at work, but I was also enduring one of the most challenging periods in my personal life, recovering from a broken engagement and adjusting to the solitude of an empty nest without the nearby support of friends or family.

Additionally, I battled constant exhaustion caused by troublesome uterine fibroids that led to prolonged periods of excessive bleeding, leaving me tired, depressed, anemic, and experiencing significant hair loss. As I combed my hair in the mornings, cleaning up the fallen strands, I found myself contemplating the purpose of my life and my will to carry on.

Along with these struggles, I felt frustrated with myself for lacking the energy to achieve as I once had. I longed for validation from my manager, yearned for a close circle of supportive friends, and, without even realizing it, was starving for self-love.

I wondered why I had dedicated most of my life to my work only to end up alone in a foreign land. Why had I made such an effort to fit in only to feel completely disconnected from both work and family? During this time, I found myself reevaluating my values and priorities.

I deeply regretted not spending more time with my daughter before she left home to pursue her career and independence. Reflecting on other relationships, including my two marriages, subsequent divorces, and the tumultuous end to my engagement, brought deep sadness. I lamented not having cultivated loving, enduring relationships in my life and wondered if I would ever learn.

Even though I took pride in my ability to build relationships in my professional spheres, I didn't know how to cultivate intimate, close relationships. I decided I wanted to live my life differently—a life where I could forge deep and authentic relationships in my personal life.

I was forced to confront my deepest fears and insecurities as I experienced this midlife crisis. I embarked on a journey to unravel the purpose of my existence and the stories that shaped my life. As I faced the pain and loneliness I had long suppressed, the narrative of my past became increasingly prominent.

## FINDING INNER STRENGTH TO PURSUE MY PURPOSE

It became increasingly difficult to show up at work. In team meetings, my voice fell silent, and I felt incapable of making valuable contributions. I felt misunderstood and lacked motivation, which caused me to struggle to perform effectively in my job.

This feeling of inadequacy also began affecting my work as a freelance coach in my part-time business. I experienced profound disappointment in myself when anxiety took over during one of the workshops I facilitated for a corporate client. It shook my confidence and left me unsure about pursuing my business full-time. Ultimately, I knew it was time for a change and finally decided to seek guidance from a career coach to explore new job opportunities.

I was worried not having a bachelor's degree would hinder my chances of getting the job I desired, despite having several professional certifications and completing college courses that directly supported my roles. Not having a degree became a haunting reminder of another one of my inner narratives, the "not good enough." Speaking with my career coach, Nick, gave me the confidence to explore industries beyond banking by aligning my previous experience with the necessary requirements for those new roles. He also recommended I enhance some of my skills by suggesting suitable training opportunities to position myself better in the job market.

Looking back on my previous employment experiences, including the freelance work I pursued through my own business, I gained the self-assurance needed to apply for the jobs I had targeted in my career search. An interesting shift occurred as I progressed through interviews and envisioned myself in those roles: I grew confident in my ability to excel in any of them. This led me to ponder the possibility of devoting myself full-time to my own business instead.

I had a realization: "If I truly believe in my capacity to excel in any of these roles, and I am willing to invest the effort to enhance my skills, why not apply the same mindset to my business?" It dawned on me that my journey of disengagement in the workplace could provide valuable insights to assist leaders in cultivating more inclusive and engaging work environments. I gathered faith and courage within me to take the leap and say, "Yes, I can do this. I will find a way." For the first time in my professional career, I was keenly aware that my heart was leading the path.

In August 2022, I made the life-altering choice to depart from my corporate job—my safety net—to pursue my business full-time. It felt similar to the decision I had made to leave my homeland of Colombia a couple of decades earlier. It became evident to me that I was not only driven to seek purposeful work but also yearned to truly experience life, embrace love, and savor the simple joys it offers.

I now understand my way of serving others did not always benefit my well-being. I often demanded a lot of myself, neglecting my needs and spreading myself too thin. I worked long hours, sometimes even skipping meals. My self-worth relied solely on external validation and the impact I had on others. My focus on my career and community service overshadowed my commitment to personal relationships.

I wondered where my lack of self-love originated from. Why was it so difficult for me to hold space and be kind to myself in the most difficult moments of my life? And why couldn't I extend love and acceptance to those closest to me? I now understand true love can only be given when we embody it ourselves. By loving and accepting who we are, we create the capacity to love and accept others unconditionally without expecting anything in return.

We all yearn to live a meaningful life. For many of us, our work and careers play a vital role in providing that sense of purpose. I believe leaders should understand what matters to their team members, recognizing, leveraging, and celebrating the talents and passions of each individual within the organization. When we feel acknowledged and valued by our leaders, we become engaged in our work and motivated to go the extra mile to fulfill the organization's goals.

As you turn the pages that follow, let's travel back a few decades into my past. There, you will encounter a younger version of myself navigating the uncertainties of life in Colombia and doing the best I could.

## Mindfulness Moment

When life feels overwhelming, find comfort in moments of stillness. Gently place your hand over your heart, close your eyes, and tune into your breath. Let go of any judgment you may hold. Remind yourself we are all doing our best with the awareness we have in each moment. As you focus on your breath, invite peace and clarity into your being. With each exhale, release any stress or tension, allowing it to melt away. In this space of stillness, hold compassion for yourself, knowing that you, too, are doing your best in each moment. The journey toward inner peace and belonging begins and ends with love—love for yourself, love for others, and love for the diversity of our human experience.

# The Struggle Is the Gift

*Compassion is one of the few things
we can practice that will bring immediate
and long-term happiness to our lives.*

—DALAI LAMA

Whether we know it or not, our upbringing shapes the way we show up in life. Doing the inner work necessary to have a greater understanding of our self-imposed limitations is up to us. Becoming aware of the stories that shape us allows us to gain the power to rewrite more empowering stories for ourselves.

Working on healing is a lifelong journey that requires acceptance and compassion for ourselves and others. The more we resist our past—and what has happened to us—the more it will continue to control our lives unconsciously.

## THE STRUGGLE

Dressed in black—a color that gave me confidence—from head to toe, I walked into the family gathering with a sense of heaviness. I felt anger. I didn't want to be there. Many members of my family were strangers to me; even as some had shown me kindness, many of them had made me feel invisible, inadequate, and stupid.

So, there I was, seventeen years old, at a family gathering. I thought I had left behind all the misery of my childhood. Working a full-time job, I proudly supported my mother and sister. I remembered my mom begging me to be kind to my grandmother, the one who had abandoned her, but I couldn't bring myself to give her the hug she so desperately desired. Sadly, my mom had her own painful tale of neglect and abuse. I held so much anger that I am fairly certain everyone there noticed.

I overheard a conversation between two of my aunts. They were looking at one of my cousins when one said, "Look how kind and beautiful she is," while the other replied, "She was raised with love." I didn't fully comprehend what that meant back then, but I understood nothing had changed for me. I was still the daughter of the "black sheep" of the family and all that came with it.

During my upbringing, I often found myself dwelling in the residences of relatives as well as unfamiliar faces, constantly grappling with a sense of being an outsider. Deep within, I carried the awareness I did not truly *belong* anywhere. I was aware of my father's existence, but he was not a consistent presence in my life. I would only see him a few times during a good year. Out of consideration for his family, he didn't publicly acknowledge me until I was an adult. My father was already married and had children when he met my mom, which is why I don't carry his name.

In Latin American culture, children commonly have two last names, for example, Martinez-Garcia, the first being your father's last name and the second coming from your mother. This became an issue for me as I encountered much criticism for not having two last names. Every time I was asked to provide my legal name, I was met with strange looks and confusion. They would say things like "What do you mean you don't have a second last name?" That question forced me to admit my father never gave me his last name, a confession that came with a sense of shame. It felt like I was revealing the most intimate parts of my life to each stranger who asked.

At the age of ten, I experienced a deep sense of abandonment when my mother brought me to a group home called Hogar de la Joven, which was an institutionalized residence managed by a convent and served as a home for up to fifty girls between the ages of ten and eighteen. These girls either came from low-income backgrounds or had behavioral issues. My mother worked as a live-in maid and was fired after getting pregnant with another absent father. Having no place to live and lacking the financial means to take care of me, my mother was forced to put me in the group home.

Adjusting to this new life was difficult as it came with strict rules and a cold environment, yet it provided the stability and discipline I needed to finish school. Growing up with my mother, I endured some of the consequences of her suffering as she would hit me with a lot of anger and desperation, and I was the only one she could discharge her anger with.

Although life with her was challenging, she was the only family and emotional connection I had.

During my mother's first visit, I threw myself at her feet, begging her to rescue me from that place. After that visit, I didn't see her for months, and I felt abandoned. The loneliness I felt intensified when other girls would leave with their parents or relatives for the weekend while I remained behind without any plans or visits from family. Over time, I accepted that was my new home.

During my first year at the group home, I faced many challenges. I initially misbehaved with the hope of being kicked out, but it only got me punished. As time passed, I grew tired of such actions and decided to abide by the rules. It wasn't until three decades later that I found out my mother never stopped visiting. Upon asking, she said, "I came every Sunday, but the nuns wouldn't let me see you. Sometimes months would pass, and due to your frequent punishments, you couldn't have visitors."

The first time my father recognized me as his daughter in front of his family was when I was twenty-four years old. My father became very ill from liver cancer and, believing he was going to die, asked me to visit him in the hospital. That visit was also the first time I was in the same space with my half sisters.

My father gazed at me with tired, yellowed eyes, a result of the anemia brought on by his illness. With a weak yet affectionate voice, he said, "I am so proud of you. You have overcome so many difficulties, even though I wasn't there for you when you needed me the most."

I replied, "But every one of your visits has been significant to me. Each of them, though infrequent, had a profound impact on my life, especially when you came bearing a pile of books, speaking to me about the importance of education and a successful career."

Before I could even utter "I love you"—as it wasn't easy for me to say those words back then—he began to feel unwell and asked me to call the nurse. I left the hospital room to let my sisters know we needed a nurse, but they ignored me. I was invisible; none of them would see me or hear me that day. They were in denial that I was there. I think the situation was likely too painful for them to admit their father had another daughter, the product of an affair.

Upon reflection, I realize the profound impact these experiences have had on my adult life. I spent seven years living in the group home run by nuns, adhering to the rigidity of that institution, which created a pattern of compliance that persisted throughout my life. I developed a tendency to be excessively self-critical and constantly berate myself. It also shaped me into an individual who strives to adhere to societal expectations, many times to the extreme.

## UNDERSTANDING MY YOUNGER SELF

During my early twenties, my Aunt Julia introduced me to the enlightening works of Dr. Wayne Dyer and Deepak Chopra. Their teachings instilled in me a profound hope during challenging times. I discovered my present circumstances did not determine my future, and I began to envision a brighter tomorrow.

Among all my aunts, she stood out as the one I admired the most. Being the youngest, she possessed an irresistible charisma, independence, and a profound love for literature. During my high school years, Julia generously provided me with the books I needed, fostering a deep connection between us. Equally warmhearted was my Uncle Francisco, whose infectious joy and radiant smile never failed to touch my soul. They had qualities I deeply admired and always wanted to emulate.

I found myself gravitating toward Julia and Francisco and others who possessed similar qualities. At the same time, I was unknowingly distancing myself from my mother, who constantly saw herself as a victim and carried a heavy sadness with her. I knew I wanted to be a better daughter, but I didn't understand why having a healthy relationship with her was so difficult.

As I was digging through old notebooks and journals, I found an entry from an ethics class and a love and forgiveness workshop when I was nineteen where I was regretting not being kind enough to my mother.

May 13, 1996—Ethics class, Servicio Nacional de Aprendizaje (SENA)

---

**WHO IS THE MOST IMPORTANT PERSON TO YOU? AND WHY?**

*My mom, but she wouldn't think so because sometimes I prefer sharing moments of happiness with other people, and I am not considerate or patient enough with her. I know I disrespect her a lot, and even though I am aware of that, I haven't been able to change. She gave me life; I must fight for her to somehow repay all the sacrifices she has made for me.*

July 8, 1996—Love and Forgiveness, Servicio Nacional de Aprendizaje (SENA)

---

**WHAT DID I REALIZE TODAY?**

*In the love and forgiveness workshop, I realized it is necessary to release all those suppressed feelings to obtain inner peace. Only when we bring to light what we are trying to hide can we confront it. I also learned forgiveness is crucial for love. We cannot love without knowing true forgiveness, and we cannot forgive if love does not exist.*

**WHAT CAN I IMPROVE?**

*I can improve the way I feel toward the people around me by acknowledging the value each of them holds and focusing on the love I can offer them.*

I was surprised to find these pieces of wisdom in my old notebooks. I can see that as a young woman, I understood these concepts cognitively, but I lacked the love within to be able to extend love to others. Even though I didn't learn to accept myself until decades later, I believe those classes planted a seed for the journey I am on today.

I have come to understand the importance of remaining connected to family and having an open heart to learn about who they are today and not who they were in the past. As I embrace my family and the beauty in them, I am doing the same thing for myself.

## HEALING THE INNER CHILD

Healing my inner child has not been a straight line or a single solution. From therapy, journaling, hypnosis, and more sophisticated modalities such as breath work, I have tried countless methods to make peace with the struggles of my upbringing and the limiting beliefs they forged.

Throughout the years, I have had many moments when I felt my past no longer weighed on me, only to later realize the layers of complexity on how I carried beliefs of inadequacy throughout my life, impacting my work, family, and relationship with myself. Something I did have clear in my early twenties, thanks to the personal development books I was reading at that time, was forgiveness was something I needed to do to liberate myself from pain. My forgiveness was not necessarily a gift I was giving to those who hurt me, including my mom, whom I resented for the life she gave me for many years.

Reflecting on the experiences that shaped me deeply has been crucial for my healing. I now have more compassion for my younger, inexperienced self and recognize I'm still learning and evolving every day. This understanding has also allowed me to have greater compassion toward others.

Dr. Paul Gilbert, a psychologist and founder of compassion-focused therapy, describes compassion as three different abilities, which he calls the Three Flows of Compassion.

**Giving compassion:** Offering support and care to another person or group who is suffering.

**Receiving compassion:** Taking in care and help when you are struggling.

**Inner compassion:** Giving compassion to yourself when you are in pain (2023).

Viewing compassion through multiple dimensions enhances our understanding of its application and benefits for personal healing and the well-being of others. Practicing compassion generously, especially in current times, is crucial for our own and collective healing.

We each face unique internal battles, and for many, these happen during our formative years. The Centers for Disease Control and Prevention (CDC) found that 61 percent of adults had at least one adverse childhood experience (ACE), which may include violence, abuse, and growing up in a family with mental health or substance use problems. The CDC also found that women and several racial/ethnic minority groups were at greater risk for experiencing four or more ACEs (2021).

Developing compassion for ourselves and others requires acknowledging that everyone is doing their best with the tools and awareness they have at any given moment. Adopting this mindset frees us from expectations that often result in pain and allows us to support others by offering understanding. Embracing a compassionate approach toward others fosters inner peace.

Today, as I interact with my relatives in new, loving ways I was unable to before, I find more uplifting memories of my younger self. Due to my pain, I had not only buried many bad memories from the past but good ones too. As I look at my life in a new light, I rewrite my personal story in ways that let me identify the gifts life has given me. Among those are the gifts of resilience and compassion.

Parenting our inner child is a lifelong journey that allows us to mend past versions of ourselves. I now recognize various aspects of my younger self manifesting in ways that may not promote well-being. I pause and address that part of me with gratitude, saying, "Thank you for sharing your fear; I will guide us to safety." Viewing internal conflicts as distinct parts of ourselves enables us to analyze our thoughts objectively and embrace the virtues of our younger selves. These virtues encompass innocence, playfulness, spontaneity, and authenticity. In our youth, we were less burdened by life's challenges, making it easier to embrace our authentic selves.

## INNER BATTLES TAKE DIFFERENT SHAPES

During a neurolinguistic programming (NLP) course in 2014, one of my classmates volunteered for a regression exercise. While sitting at the front of the classroom, Samantha allowed the facilitator to guide her through a series of questions, delving into her upbringing to uncover the root cause of her present unhappiness. As she shared her experience of growing up in a loving and harmonious middle-class family, I was taken aback by how any of it could have contributed to her current suffering.

However, Samantha revealed her struggle in her marriage stemmed from her inability to establish boundaries and assert herself, hindering her from recreating the happy home she remembered from her childhood. The realization was powerful for me, and I understood how our individual lived experiences can manifest as trauma or challenges that impede our ability to create fulfilling lives.

Samantha spoke of her parents, exemplifying their care and togetherness, which appeared to create an ideal home I never had. She never witnessed her parents argue, and she strove to emulate that perfect home, but by avoiding conflict, she experienced dissatisfaction in her marriage. It surprised me that even with a stable family dynamic and two dedicated parents, she struggled to create a happy life for herself.

I wondered if their perfect home was perhaps a facade, concealing constant arguments behind closed doors, or one of them silently suffering, always accommodating the other's needs. Although I will never know the reality of her family situation, one thing became clear: The experiences and traumas we carry from childhood, regardless of how others perceive them, can inflict genuine pain and struggles upon us.

In February 2023, I crossed paths with Alejandro Juan Marcos at a Deepak Chopra retreat in San José del Cabo, Mexico. During one of the sessions at this transformative weeklong event, we engaged in deep conversations, sharing reflections and offering feedback. Alejandro exuded a sense of joy and peace, making our interactions truly delightful. Our connection extended beyond the retreat, prompting me to inquire about his journey. I said, "I love the way you carry yourself. Do you have a self-love story?" He smiled and shared it with me. I was surprised to learn about his struggle to accept himself a few years earlier. Here is the story he shared with me:

*I was twenty-five years old when, due to threats from my ex-partner, I came out to my parents. Being in a Mexican, ultra-religious family, this task was not easy.*

*My family locked me in my house for months. They forbade me from going to work by myself; my brother had to drop me off and pick me up. I couldn't see my friends, and I lost my freedom.*

*For three years, I was in this dynamic where, out of fear, I surrendered my power and self-love. I let my family dictate what gave me value and what took it away. I believed them when they told me if I showed my authentic self to society, I would be rejected, left alone, and become the mockery of my city.*

*As with everything in life, nothing is permanent. My state of 'victim' came to an end when, on a trip with my friends, I decided to bet on myself and ask for their support. I told them about what I was going through and that I truly understood if they no longer wanted to be my friends, but I didn't want to continue pretending with the people I cared about.*

*To my surprise, everyone accepted me in an incredible way, and they encouraged me to move forward and included me more than ever.*

*Thanks to the support of my friends, I left my parents' house, had my first healthy relationship, and, above all, took control of my life.*

*I learned three things in this process.*

*First, no matter how much you love the people in your life, sacrificing your life for others is not healthy. In Latin cultures, we are taught family is the most important thing we have. But they don't tell us that family can also be toxic people to us. Sometimes, we have to take a step back even if it hurts.*

*Second, although we may not realize it, we are one decision away from changing our lives. We can be very comfortable within our discomfort, but in that place, we do not evolve. It depends on us if we want to give a new chapter to our story.*

*And finally, we always have people who can support us and people with whom we can build community. If one day you have to help, do it from the heart. You never know the true impact you can have on others' lives—from smiling at a stranger on the street to inspiring someone to take control of their life, as my friends did with me.*

The healing journey may be painful, but the journey is worth the effort as it leads us to a life of more inner peace and healthier relationships with others.

Trauma subtly integrates into our very essence, changing how we perceive the world, interact with others, and view ourselves. Often, we go through life unaware of the profound impact our upbringing or challenging life events have on us. By reflecting on and processing these pivotal experiences, we can better understand and empathize with the life stories of others. To empower those around us, reaffirming their inherent worth and supporting their path to self-acceptance is important.

# Mindfulness Moment

Nurturing your inner child requires a conscious decision to heal from past wounds. Though it may seem overwhelming, practicing mindfulness can guide you to integrate all aspects of yourself. Begin by creating a safe space to connect with the part of you that still carries pain. Allow yourself to experience emotions without judgment or resistance. Validate your feelings, and remember mourning what might have been is natural. Envision love and acceptance flowing in as you inhale, while releasing any judgment and negativity as you exhale. Through the grieving process, we can liberate ourselves from pain and reach a point where we recognize how our past experiences have shaped our character, granting us invaluable insights. As you continue your healing journey, you'll discover you're not only cultivating self-love but also becoming a conscious leader of your own life.

# CHAPTER 3

# In Search of a Better Life

---

*Life is either a daring adventure
or nothing at all.*

—HELEN KELLER

I realized I couldn't possibly explain my decision to my three-year-old daughter in a way she could fully comprehend. So, I looked into her eyes and said, "Mommy won't be around for a while, but Mommy loves you very, very much. I won't be here with you, but Mommy always loves you. Mommy will be back; you mean the world to me." I repeated these words, hoping they would etch themselves into her memory and she would always remember the depth of my love for her.

Leaving my native land of Colombia in 2002 and embarking on a journey to the United States was an incredibly difficult decision, but it ignited a flicker of hope within me. During those dark days, I felt utterly lost and didn't know who I was. I internalized all the verbal abuse I endured from my husband—a reminder of unconscious beliefs from childhood. "You are too skinny, too stupid, too clueless," the recurring message echoed, a constant reinforcement of my sense of inadequacy.

## A DIFFICULT DECISION

One afternoon, when my daughter Valerie was one year old, my husband, Juan, noticed she was struggling to breathe due to a cold. He acted quickly, getting extra pillows to position them under her head and back and elevating her in the crib to improve her breathing. His disappointment in me at that moment was evident and something I became used to as he continuously accused me of neglecting her well-being. Although I was doing the best I could, not knowing things that seemed so basic to him left me overwhelmed with shame and guilt. I was twenty-one years old when I had Val. I was young and inexperienced. Unlike my husband, I was not well-versed in these situations and did not have firsthand experience with nieces and nephews.

Juan would be deeply concerned if Val happened to sustain any small scratches or bruises while exploring the world as a toddler. I used to fear something might happen to her, mostly due to his reaction, especially on the days I was working and my mom was taking care of her. We knew how upset he could get if anything happened to her, and we dreaded having to deal with his reaction. Juan, who was thirteen years older than me, was at a point in his life where he considered having a child as being the most important thing he could do, so he became overly protective of her.

Although he was a devoted father, he was not the best husband. His care and affection toward me were limited to our dating years, which lasted a total of four. Our marriage, on the other hand, only lasted three years. The downfall of the marriage stemmed from a lack of understanding and communication, among many other things. I had failed to communicate my needs from the beginning and tolerated his mistreatment for far too long until reaching my breaking point. My subsequent outbursts of anger ultimately extinguished the love in our marriage.

Juan's expectations of a good wife were confined to someone who stayed at home and took care of the house and children, but that person wasn't me. I was naive and unprepared to build a healthy relationship where I could express my own needs within a marriage. We wanted different things, and I lacked the ability to articulate my aspirations before committing to marrying him.

For my high school graduation and prior to getting married, Juan gave me a big bouquet of flowers with a handwritten note that said, "Congratulations on one of many achievements to come!" With this note, I naively assumed he would always support me, yet I never told him of my dreams of pursuing higher education and a career. At the time, I didn't know how to have a serious conversation about what I wanted, and I was so worried about pleasing everyone else that I didn't prioritize my own needs.

Juan finally granted me the divorce after I assured him I would leave with nothing—no possessions or child support—but with the promise he would buy everything Val needed. Despite us being divorced, I continued to endure verbal abuse and control from him. He closely monitored every move I made and questioned my work schedule and decisions. Eventually, he pressured me to move to a more affluent neighborhood, away from low-income families, despite the strain it caused on my finances.

The exorbitant cost of housing in the new neighborhood would leave me with insufficient funds to cover the essential items for my twelve-year-old sister and our mother, whom I also provided for and who lived with me. On some occasions, we didn't have enough money for even a basic meal. On one desperate occasion, I reached out to Juan, seeking assistance with food. I will never forget that day when he arrived with a single piece of chicken, intended for us to make soup for Val. While I was grateful for having food for my daughter, I couldn't ignore the harsh reality that the rest of us would not have anything to eat that day. That day was a stark reminder that my current situation was not sustainable, and I saw no way out.

Ana, a coworker who was the closest thing I had to a friend, witnessed my tears on several occasions, watching me suffer in my marriage and struggle financially after the divorce. She had mentioned on multiple occasions that if I ever wanted to go to the United States, her brother, who already lived there, could help me. However, the thought of leaving without my daughter was inconceivable, so I never seriously considered it.

Lucy, another colleague at the factory, wanted nothing more than to move to the US to reunite with her husband but was unable to obtain her visa. She was distraught when she got rejected and confided in Ana that her visa was denied. I happened to walk into Ana's office when she turned to Lucy and said, "Claudia has a US visa, and she doesn't want to go." Traveling to the US was Juan's dream, not mine. Back then, it took years to even get an appointment when applying for a visa, so Juan had made one for us and our daughter when we were together. Lucy couldn't believe I had a visa and chose not to go and was insistent about how much better the quality of life is in the US compared to what we were living in Colombia. At that moment, everything she said sounded intriguing, and it gave me some hope for my future.

I had a very limited understanding of the US, particularly of the immigrant experience or the economy, but everything Lucy presented sounded promising. She highlighted the potential to earn a higher income, purchase a car, and save money, all of which I considered to be luxuries. Even small conveniences like everyone having a microwave at home were intriguing. Amid all her insights, all I could think of was the opportunities for growth, independence, and the promise of a new life. It wasn't until that conversation that I truly started considering what it would be like to embark on a journey to the US to pursue a better life.

The anticipation of moving to the US brought about similar emotions as when I finally left the group home. I was seventeen and felt a newfound sense of independence and believed I could achieve anything. I felt an immense sense of pride that I was able to bring my family back together. I was seventeen, and it was the first time my mother, sister, and I lived under one roof in our own home.

During my marriage, I had lost touch with my drive and ability to dream, but after finally deciding to move to the US, the spark of hope and possibility for the future was reignited. Leaving my daughter behind was an incredibly difficult choice, but I took comfort in knowing Juan would provide excellent care and she would be surrounded by family who loved her. I armed myself with a renewed self-belief and a newfound determination to create a better life for my daughter and me. So I took a leap of faith and fearlessly embarked on a journey into the unknown.

## LANDING IN A LAND OF HOPE

I landed in Providence, Rhode Island, on a hot August summer day in 2002 with $500 in my pocket and a dream. To fund my trip, I sold my bright yellow Suzuki Address, the faithful scooter that transported me for years and the only thing I ever owned. After buying my flight tickets, $500 and a small suitcase of essentials were all I had left. Upon my arrival in the US, unaware of the time zone difference, I missed my connecting flight from Miami to Providence. I was able to reschedule my flight for the next day, although I had to spend my first night sleeping in the airport.

Daniel, Ana's brother, was my only contact, and he could no longer pick me up from the Providence airport since he had taken the previous day off work to do so. I attempted to reach him through a public phone but struggled to do so because I didn't know how to dial domestic calls since I had only called him from Colombia.

I had a piece of paper with the words "Latin Grilled Chicken" written on them. Daniel worked there, and I was determined to get there on my own. I approached taxi drivers and showed them my piece of paper, hoping they knew exactly where I needed to go, but I kept getting dismissed by a loud, "I need an address." After multiple failed attempts, I finally found a Spanish-speaking driver and felt safe again. He recognized the name and kindly let me know the restaurant I was looking for was just a stand in the food court of a local mall.

I found myself at the Providence mall, searching for Daniel and the hidden Mexican restaurant where he worked. I felt so overwhelmed attempting to navigate such a large and unfamiliar mall that even using the electric stairs with a suitcase intimidated me. I held on to my suitcase tight but was too afraid to place it on the moving steps until someone noticed me struggling and kindly pointed toward the right elevator. On the way, I relied on gestures and showed strangers my scrap piece of paper with the restaurant's name to reach my destination.

I felt relieved when I finally arrived at Daniel's workplace. He warmly greeted me and offered me some food, and I patiently waited for his shift to end. Later that evening, upon reaching his apartment, I met his roommate. Both Daniel and Carlos were kind and welcoming. Their presence filled me with immense gratitude for a safe landing and the companionship of trustworthy individuals.

Within days, Daniel arranged an interview with the restaurant's manager for me. Despite the language barrier, I landed the job, thanks to Daniel's credibility with the manager. Daniel told me, "Claudia, you struggled with Lee's basic questions. He doubted your ability to speak English and was unsure about how long you would last on the job, but he's giving you a chance." Daniel became my mentor, urging me to memorize the menu and providing invaluable guidance that ultimately secured me the position.

After a couple of months, I realized I needed to find a new place to call home. Daniel had confessed he had feelings for me and even proposed that we move to Canada together, where the prospects for immigrants were more promising. However, I declined his offer, and our friendship took a strange turn.

One chilly autumn day, as I made my way to the laundromat a few blocks away, it hit me that my time at Daniel's house had run its course. I was overcome with a sense of fear and uncertainty about where to go next. The unfamiliar cold air made my hands stiff as I struggled to insert quarters into the washing machine, only to realize it was already full of coins. Overwhelmed by a flood of emotions, I leaned against the machine with tears streaming down my face.

In a moment of divine intervention, a kind-hearted Guatemalan woman, who must have been in her seventies, placed her hand on my shoulder and asked if I needed a place to stay. Through this serendipitous encounter, I found myself moving into her home just days later. Doña Alba and her daughter, Margarita, provided me with safe refuge.

I would work seven days a week and take English classes every weeknight at the Lutheran church across from the mall. Not only did I improve my English skills there, but I also found a supportive community. It provided comfort and a sense of belonging, allowing me to connect with other immigrants facing similar challenges as newcomers to the US.

One of my most loyal customers, a tall American with a bright smile, began showing more interest in me than the burritos he bought every Friday afternoon. After a few dates, we entered a serious relationship that led to him becoming my second husband.

In 2004, with the support of my then-husband Tom, I completed a six-month insurance technician program at Rhode Island College and eventually obtained my property and casualty license. The program demanded my full-time dedication as I tackled insurance terminology while simultaneously mastering the English language, making it an incredibly challenging endeavor. I recall recording the classes and diligently reviewing them at home, armed with my insurance book and my digital English translator, which I carried everywhere. I was grateful for Tom's support in championing my professional growth and sponsoring my daughter's visa, which eventually enabled her to live with me in the United States years later.

## A MEMORABLE REUNION AND CELEBRATION

I arranged for my daughter, accompanied by her father, to visit me. Together, we celebrated my graduation from Rhode Island College on June 30, 2004. During the time I was apart from my daughter, Juan lovingly cared for her. His understanding of the importance of a mother's presence and his love for her enabled our reunion.

As I looked into the audience, gratitude overwhelmed me. Beside me stood my five-year-old daughter and her father, marking this significant occasion. This event held immense significance as it represented my triumph over numerous challenges and my dedication to learning English. Above all, it filled my heart with immense pride to have fulfilled my promise to be reunited with my daughter after two years of not seeing her.

A few years later, when Val obtained her residency, Juan and I shared responsibilities during vacations and the school year, raising her together in both countries and shaping her into a bicultural and bilingual individual.

## EMPOWERMENT THROUGH MENTORSHIP

During a community meeting near my employer's office, I had the privilege of listening to Sixcia Devine speak about the programs and services provided at the Center for Women & Enterprise (CWE), an organization committed to increasing women's economic empowerment through entrepreneurship. Sixcia was eloquent in her speech and had a captivating smile and a magnetic personality. Determined to connect with her, I rushed my way through the crowd of merchants, reaching her before she departed in her vehicle from the parking lot.

Approaching her, I handed her my business card and introduced myself. A few weeks later, I had the opportunity to meet with her at her office. During our meeting, she asked, "What aspects do you enjoy the most about your job?" I expressed to her that what I enjoyed the most about my role was educating consumers about their options and providing policies that offered value to them. I also let her know it was difficult for me to sell policies when I knew my customers could have access to more affordable plans somewhere else.

A few days later, I received a call from Sixcia. She said, "Claudia, I have the perfect job for you. Come to my office." Intrigued, I eagerly made my way to her office. As I entered, Sixcia handed me a document containing the job description. I found myself struggling to fully grasp the various terms and overall job requirements, as the world of business was still relatively unfamiliar to me at that time.

Seeing my confusion, Sixcia reassured me. "Claudia, you don't understand. They need you. They need someone like you who has built a reputation in the Latino community. You would be a bridge between the state's business resources and Latino merchants and immigrants looking to start new ventures. You will get to do the customer service you enjoy, and the community will benefit from having someone like you."

To further prepare me for the interview, Sixcia gave me an SBA magazine listing all the business resources in the state. She also coached me, helped me write my résumé and cover letter, and conducted a mock interview. She was like an angel guiding me on my next professional journey.

Like many immigrants who made incredible sacrifices to lay a path for future generations, I endured heartache from being apart from my daughter and family in those early years, but I recognized the opportunities before me and bravely faced the challenges. My journey was not just a physical transition from Colombia to the United States but also a voyage of self-discovery.

Workplace leaders have the power to make a significant difference in the lives of individuals by creating an inclusive environment that celebrates their unique stories and resilience, nurtures their talent, and fosters their growth. It is essential for leaders to actively listen, offer mentorship, and provide tailored professional development opportunities that recognize and address the unique obstacles employees may face. By championing diversity, ensuring equitable access to resources, and fostering a culture of openness and support, leaders can empower every member of their team to achieve their best.

## Mindfulness Moment

Each of us has a unique story, a personal voyage shaped by our experiences, choices, and the people we meet along the way. Take a moment to reflect on your journey. Embrace your emotions without judgment and observe the feelings that arise. Ground yourself by connecting with the earth beneath your feet, relaxing your shoulders and face, and releasing any tension in your jaw. Say thank you to your younger self for the challenging decisions that have molded you, and acknowledge the lessons and resilience they have instilled in you. Stay mindful of your breath for a few minutes and cherish your growth.

# Transformational Trips: A Journey to Self

*The real voyage of discovery consists not in seeking new landscapes but in having new eyes.*

—MARCEL PROUST

In the winter of 2021, I felt disconnected and overwhelmed by profound loneliness. The new life I had built for my daughter and me in the United States was no longer a source of purpose. Valerie had already embarked on her own path across the country, carving out her own destiny.

As a mother, I felt a deep sense of fulfillment. I knew my daughter possessed the determination to thrive in her new corporate role, which she proudly secured after graduating from college. And I also felt proud of her kind and compassionate nature. I knew she had the foresight to create a good life for herself.

So there I was, an empty nester pondering what was next for me and already feeling a sense of disconnection at work, which for a long time also gave me a deep sense of meaning in life. Amid the uncertainty, something was clear to me: I needed a new purpose in life, and I was determined to find it. At that point, I made the life-changing decision to join an Ayahuasca ceremony with the Pasto indigenous tribe in Colombia.

Ayahuasca is a potent brew crafted mainly from the leaves of the Psychotria viridis shrub and the stalks of the Banisteriopsis caapi vine, both native to the Amazon rainforest. When combined, these plants create a potent psychedelic blend that triggers an altered state of consciousness. Historically, ancient Amazonian tribes utilized this brew for spiritual and religious purposes. Today, certain religious communities in Brazil and North America, like the Santo Daime, continue to embrace Ayahuasca as a sacred beverage (Kubala 2022).

While watching a Gaia documentary, I came across Ayahuasca, known as the "vine of the soul." Gaia, a conscious media platform, offers mind-expanding films and documentaries. After extensive research on this plant, known as Yagé in Colombia, I decided to explore it despite uncertainties. Seekers pursue this medicine for healing, purpose, and spiritual connection. Though side effects like purging are common, those dedicated to healing and growth embrace the challenges. Testimonials focus on profound insights and transformative experiences rather than pleasure, highlighting personal quests and confronting unsettling visions.

## AYAHUASCA, AN UNEXPECTED JOURNEY WITHIN

With faith in Ayahuasca's ability to provide insight into my life's purpose, I embarked on this journey. Feeling lost at the time, I was determined to understand my path. Despite reservations rooted in their religious beliefs, my mother, sister, and brother-in-law honored my decision and drove me to the sacred ceremony. I was pleasantly surprised to discover the Pasto indigenous tribe was situated merely an hour away from my sister's residence. Although I had considered attending ceremonies in other regions of Colombia or possibly Peru, it felt like a sign that I was destined to participate in the ceremony in the small province of Quindío, where I was born. Having my family by my side played a significant role in the subtle answers I gleaned from the experience.

As the ceremony neared, despite being just an hour away from my family's home, we found ourselves in a remote area with a narrow path that allowed only one car to pass at a time. Each encounter with a vehicle heading in the opposite direction led to a graceful tilt of one car at a thirty-degree angle into the embankment while the other navigated skillfully around it. This created a sense of anticipation within me as we drew closer to my destination.

I checked in at the front of the house before descending a staircase that led me to a magnificent bamboo gazebo nestled amid the untamed trees, shrubs, and wildflowers.

Upon entering the gazebo, I scanned the thin mattresses scattered across the floor, searching for my name. I observed the diverse array of individuals, many of whom were elegantly dressed in white, possibly hailing from different parts of the country. Among them, I discerned a few tourists, predominantly Americans, easily recognizable by their conversations.

As we entered the night, approximately fifty individuals lay on the floor, nestled amid pillows and blankets. The sacred space was cleansed ceremoniously with the fragrant smoke of burning dried sage. Thoughtful volunteers handed each of us plastic bags, a small comfort in case we needed them. The shaman, or Taita as we Colombians prefer to call this wise person with expansive ancestral knowledge, led each of us to embark on a journey of connection. Listening intently, he sought to understand our ailments, concerns, and even the medications we were taking despite our diligent adherence to the preparation guidelines, including a light vegetarian diet in the preceding days. The Taita took time to listen to each of us personally, offering blessings for the transformative night ahead.

When the Taita approached me, his gaze met mine, and he inquired about the purpose that led me there that evening. I confided in him, sharing my feelings of being lost in regard to my life's purpose. I found solace in the way he spoke, emanating wisdom and kindness.

Close to midnight, the prayers and chants started, followed by the Ayahuasca medicine served in very small cups and drunk by the altar. The Ayahuasca medicine was thick and difficult to swallow, and I drank mine as fast as I could, immediately followed by water. I went to my mattress, got under my blanket, closed my eyes, and faithfully waited for the clear vision of my future and life's purpose.

After a couple of hours and intensive ruminating in my mind, I vomited into the plastic bag I had placed under my pillow. I felt relieved afterward. As I lay on the mat, I experienced disappointment that I hadn't experienced something "significant" or "profound"—no new realizations about my life. I could see and hear others crying, even screaming. A couple of interventions required several volunteers to hold individuals who were moving desperately around their visions and struggles in their Ayahuasca journey.

Not me. I was still in my head, reflecting on my life, the ups and downs, and pondering why my vision for the future remained elusive. The chanting and beautiful live instrumental music were a delight. I would open my eyes multiple times that night, convinced someone was singing and playing instruments right beside me. But I believe the high ceiling and rounded shape of the gazebo created that effect. I remember moments when fear consumed me, and I thought the sounds of nature outside the gazebo posed a threat to my safety.

In the morning, I felt alive and energized despite only having had about an hour of sleep. I shared some of the fruit I had brought with the spiritual seekers nearby, and we exchanged our experiences from the previous evening's journey. I felt a deep sense of connection with them on our paths. The integration ceremony that morning lasted until noon, encompassing a couple of hours of prayer, drums, singing, and blessings. I had another chance to talk to the Taita and discuss my sadness about not having a vision. He reassured me it was okay and explained that the Ayahuasca was facilitating the necessary cleansing for my healing process.

As my sister and her husband picked me up in their car, I reflected on my experience and shared a few details with them about the evening's ceremony. When we arrived at my sister's home, Mom was already cooking. She had waited for us to return so we could have lunch together.

Despite feeling exhausted and thinking about how much I wanted to go to sleep, I stopped in the kitchen to acknowledge my mom and express how grateful I was for her making us lunch and for her constant efforts to serve others. The warmth in my heart compelled me to let her know how much I valued her efforts.

With a big smile on her face, she stepped into the living room, a bigger space for her to freely open her arms and pour out her emotions. She said, "It is very important to me to do something for others every day. The day I don't serve someone, I feel like I didn't truly live that day." At that moment, I saw her with new eyes and finally understood her and what she stood for.

It dawned on me that her own desire to be of service was a gift she had passed down to me. I find fulfillment and joy in serving others.

My life story about my mom was mostly about the bad choices she made in her life and how they affected me. But in that moment, I felt immense love and respect for her and everything she did for me and my sister with the limited resources she had. I no longer judged her; I felt pure love for my mother and who she was.

Looking back, I now understand why I never had grandiose visions during my Ayahuasca journey. The sacred plants knew exactly what I needed and spoke to me through my intellect because that was the only way I could connect at that time, and these sacred healing plants brought me into the heart in my family's presence, especially with my mom.

My experience with Ayahuasca not only deepened my love and appreciation for my family but also influenced my decision to resign from my corporate role a few months later. This spiritual journey provided me with a newfound clarity of my values, leading to a growing sense of discontent in my professional life.

While I found Ayahuasca personally enlightening, I understand it may not be suitable for everyone and do not recommend it unless individuals are genuinely drawn to exploring such practices. For those compelled to embark on this path, thorough research is essential to ensure an authentic and safe shamanic experience. South America has reputable retreat centers specializing in plant medicine. Alternatively, exploring the depths of your mind and releasing emotional barriers can also be achieved through breathwork and meditation. I believe numerous paths to discovering one's true self exist, each unique to the individual.

## IN BARCELONA: WALK, DON'T RUN

As I thought about the new life I wanted to create for myself,
I decided to travel. I reconnected with Joan, whom I had
virtually met a decade earlier. His journey intrigued me.
Leaving his corporate job in 2010, he dedicated the next eight
years of his life to creating "ULU, Un Latido Universal," an
inspiring documentary that explores what it means to live a
life guided by the heart. After updating Joan on the recent
events in my life, we began arranging the trip, and I became
excited to meet him in person.

Joan challenged me to travel light, as we would be doing
some exploring within Spain. So, I carefully selected versatile
clothing and managed to fit everything into a forty-liter
backpack for my twenty-day stay in Spain. The process of
packing only the essentials for the trip was quite challenging
yet inspirational. I had to let go of many things I considered
essential in my daily routine.

On October 17, 2022, the day of departure finally came, and
I was filled with excitement. After enduring eleven hours
of flights and layovers, I reached the airport to find Joan
waiting for me in the welcome area. A mix of nervousness
and happiness washed over me as I approached him.

Joan became my spiritual guide on a journey of self-
discovery, self-acceptance, and rewriting the narrative
of my life. As we wandered through the narrow streets
of Barcelona, delving into rich symbolism and exploring
the expansive Catalonia Square, he introduced me to a
new way of viewing the world. I learned that everything
communicates with you when you take your time, fully

present to the rhythm of your heart and the beauty surrounding you.

Our walks in the streets of Barcelona were enchanting. I cherished observing the intricately designed buildings and cathedrals by Antoni Gaudí, a renowned Spanish architect. Being curious and engaging with Joan about all the wonders I encountered was delightful. One day, his playful response made me realize something profound: I was rediscovering the world with the innocence of a little girl, feeling the nurturing fatherly energy I had longed for in my life.

Joan's influence on me during our journey was profound, and a mix of tears and laughter often overcame me. Tears flowed as I acknowledged the mental barriers I had placed on myself, hindering a fulfilling life. Laughter followed as I embraced the realization that the past was just a story and I could create a new reality for myself in the present moment.

One day, as we returned to the hotel, Joan asked me to open the door. I tried to unlock it by quickly tapping the digital key but failed. Calmly, he demonstrated, waiting for the beep before effortlessly opening the door. In that instant, it dawned on me how I had navigated much of my life. Although I had used digital keys in hotels before, the experience varied. Sometimes the doors opened easily. Other times, they didn't, and I struggled until they did. It never occurred to me that my impatience and lack of presence caused many of my struggles in life. The digital key was a metaphor for how I was living my life.

Another day, we passed by a store with a large sign of a naked woman wearing Camper shoes with the following message: Walk, Don't Run. Joan asked me to stop and look at it, and then he said, "I think these are the shoes you need." I understood what he meant right away. I had spent most of my life running from one thing to another. Even though I felt uncomfortable with the ad, I decided to walk into the store anyway. I tried a pair and felt uncomfortable with the design since they were a bit difficult to put on. When I shared my concerns with Joan, he asked, "Why the rush to put on your shoes?"

I came up with other excuses to avoid buying those shoes that day. I thought they were ridiculous shoes I wouldn't wear or let anyone see me wearing. I worried my vegan friends would be upset with me for wearing leather shoes, and my Latino friends would think they were clown shoes and make fun of me. The sales representative at the store carefully explained how the shoes were designed to allow full movement of the foot and toes as if you were walking barefoot. I left the store not fully convinced I would ever wear them, but after reflecting, I went back the next day and bought them.

Today, my Camper shoes are my favorite travel shoes. They remind me to be flexible in my thinking, be fully present every time I put them on, feel and enjoy each step in my journey, not care about what others may think about my decisions, and make choices that are good for me and bring me peace and comfort.

Every day spent with Joan was an adventure and a chance to embrace life as it came, releasing control and expectations.

Whether we were wandering the streets of Barcelona or soaking up the sun on the beaches of Menorca, it was the most incredible journey I had experienced up to that point in my life. To offer you a peek into my thoughts during those times with him, as well as my solo explorations in Barcelona, here are some excerpts from my journal.

## JOURNAL ENTRIES IN THE MEDITERRANEAN

*October 24, 2022*

*Today, Joan was not there walking with me and reminding me to embrace the natural flow of life or encouraging me to find joy in the simple surprises that every moment brings. I was doing that for myself. I let life guide me in the streets of Barcelona.*

*I ate at BO&MIE, sat on a bench observing the pigeons around, and anticipated visiting La Sagrada Familia, not fully comprehending the mystical experience that awaited me. I was glad to have taken the tourist bus to arrive there and appreciated the creative city from a different perspective.*

*October 26, 2022*

*Traveling to the Mediterranean with Joan has been quite an adventure and has surpassed all my expectations. Joan has been an incredible teacher, imparting valuable life lessons. Through his guidance, I now see myself more clearly and recognize how I projected my high expectations onto past partners instead of seeking to understand them deeply.*

*I am overflowing with love and compassion, not just for myself but for the world around me. Experiencing Barcelona and visiting Montserrat in the holy mountain has awakened a new version of Claudia Cardozo, more peaceful and loving.*

*This entire trip has immersed me in a life of abundance. I have felt what it is to have it all, enjoying love and peace. With newfound clarity, I have come to understand my essence; I am light, I am love, and I am created in the image and likeness of God.*

Joan taught me that peace and joy are possible when we embrace the flow of life and the divine that resides in each of us. I consider myself privileged to have embarked on this transformative journey of self-discovery and spiritual growth under his guidance.

## THE DOMINICAN SISTERHOOD

In December 2022, I embarked on another transformative journey, immersing myself in the enchanting Caribbean for a remarkable twenty-day experience alongside my cherished friend, Anyi (An-jee). After leaving her corporate career, she wholeheartedly embraced her passion for teaching yoga and practicing Ayurveda in the beautiful landscapes of the Dominican Republic. Our retreat took place in Casa Bienestar, a sanctuary she built amid the Caribbean mountains.

Anyi had introduced me to yoga back in 2020. We practiced together virtually once a week with a few other women from Rhode Island while Anyi was in DR. I was thrilled to be visiting her since we had been planning this trip for a long time. My days at the retreat began with personalized yoga sessions with Anyi. I told her one morning, "I could definitely get used to this every day!" I also enjoyed soothing massages and nourishing Ayurvedic meals tailored to my dosha profile. Sacred rituals and introspective journaling were the highlights of my days.

Ayurveda is an ancient holistic healing system that remains widely practiced today. It focuses on physical, psychological, and spiritual well-being, aiming to heal the entire body. Ayurveda suggests that an individual's dosha, the dynamic principle, influences their personality and health. This system is based on the belief in five elements—space, water, earth, fire, and air. The combination of these elements leads to Vata, Kapha, and Pitta, the three doshas responsible for maintaining physical, mental, and emotional balance (Davidson 2023).

I still recall the enchanting nights at Casa Bienestar, falling asleep to the serenade of frogs and crickets. Amid it all, I shared my space with a couple of playful salamanders, who would often hide behind the artwork. Although I could always spot the end of their tails, I trusted they wouldn't join me in bed. I deeply connected with nature and myself through daily healing rituals and journaling.

## JOURNAL ENTRIES IN CASA BIENESTAR, SANTO DOMINGO

*December 15, 2022*

---

*Today, I write from the terrace facing the mountains in the northern part of the Dominican Republic, in the hammock, a beautiful place of peace and contemplation. It was beautiful seeing Anyi again yesterday. I appreciate all of her preparations for my arrival and the beautiful large sunflowers she greeted me with at the airport. I felt her love. The sunflowers are now in a large Hindu vase to the right of the door of my small house, made inside a shipping container and painted blue, where I will live for the next five days.*

*December 16, 2022*

---

*As I gently swayed in the hammock, I felt a mystical experience. The birds' songs felt clearer and more memorable, and the leaves of the large tree I was observing seemed as if it was painted in the blue sky, as the wind was absent. I wondered if this was how painters saw their works before putting them on canvas and remembered a painter friend who once told me, "We paint with our eyes, not with our hands." I deeply admired nature and the artists who capture it in their works.*

During the second week, I visited Cosmic, whom Anyi had recommended me to spend time with. Cosmic was a fearless Black woman and Minnesota native with a deep sense of self and a clear purpose in life. In 2020, she acquired a piece of land in the Caribbean mountains of the Dominican Republic and established Sacred Space Village as her home and sanctuary. Her vision was to create a refuge for Black and Brown individuals seeking to disconnect from the relentless demands of modern life and embark on a journey of ancestral healing and connection to Mother Earth.

As I got to know Cosmic, I became inspired by her ability to be present and create the reality she wanted every day. When something didn't go as planned, she never lost her joy and would say, "Don't worry, Claudia, we'll have a great time," and out of nothing, she would manifest a new plan.

Cosmic was an attentive listener, giving me her undivided attention whenever we were together. After a few days, I began feeling more comfortable opening up to her in deeper ways. We delved into the reasons behind my initial hesitation to fully express myself, and we discovered my upbringing and cultural background played a significant role.

This hesitation stemmed from my need to please others and my desire to be liked. Many times, I would sacrifice my truth and voice for the benefit of others as I always aimed to be polite and say the "right thing." In contrast, from a young age, Cosmic was taught to speak up and to stand in her power. As we spent days and nights together for a whole week, we learned a lot about each other's heritage and felt a greater sense of admiration and compassion for each other's cultural differences.

I found inspiration in Cosmic, her kids, and three other empowered Black women during my time at Sacred Space Village. I felt honored to share moments with her and her community. The wisdom they imparted regarding self-care, being present, and self-awareness was precious. It transformed my outlook and profoundly enriched my life.

A few days after my stay at Sacred Space Village, Anyi, Cosmic, and I reunited. The day was truly special as we celebrated the bond of sisterhood that had blossomed between us. We did face masks, cooked together, and gave each other foot massages. Individually, we reflected on the unique contributions we brought to one another's lives. They both helped me gain a deeper understanding and acceptance of myself. Anyi encouraged me to trust myself and speak my truth. Cosmic showed me the importance of being present and acknowledged my gift of compassion.

The process of healing with other women is something I had never experienced quite like this before. Their love still carries me forward every time I remember those special and powerful encounters.

After our retreats together, I took a couple of days for myself to reflect on everything I had just experienced. I stayed in a hotel on Boca Chica Beach and decided to spend as much time as I could in nature and enjoying the Caribbean Sea. I walked across the soft white sand and released my body into the water, effortlessly floating on my back with my eyes closed. As I listened to the sounds of the ocean and birds, I felt a deep sense of peace and stillness.

After some time, I stood up and made my way back toward the shore when I saw a small fish following me. I slowed down to see if the fish would continue its course somewhere else, only to notice more fish were coming and swimming circles around me. In that extraordinary moment, I became one with the experience, feeling fully alive. It felt as if Mother Nature and I were kindred spirits, connected by an unbreakable bond. I felt a shift within me, truly appreciating the elements in nature and intimately feeling its presence.

As I neared the beach, a boy of about eight years old asked me if I was the one floating in the water. He was accompanied by a younger girl, probably six years old, who had a big smile on her face. When I confirmed to the boy that I was indeed floating in the water, he asked, "Would you teach us how to float?" Once I received permission from their parents, I enjoyed spending time with them and teaching them how to float. The bond I formed with the six-year-old girl was particularly special, creating a beautiful experience filled with a profound connection.

After that encounter with those beautiful kids, I knew a transformation was taking place in me. I was engaging with the world in new ways, enjoying each moment fully, letting life surprise me with its beauty.

Those aspiring to lead can gain tremendous insights by immersing themselves in travel experiences. These journeys cultivate open-mindedness and compassion. Rather than seeking comfort, embracing discomfort while on the road is vital. In these challenging moments beyond our comfort zones, lasting memories and priceless experiences are created. This form of travel not only introduces us to new perspectives but also challenges our assumptions, sparking creativity. It serves as a path to self-discovery and a potent means to enhance interpersonal skills by fostering a deeper understanding of diverse cultures and beliefs.

# Mindfulness Moment

When embarking on a journey, whether long or short, seize the opportunity to fully immerse yourself in the experience. Close your eyes and take a deep breath. Allow yourself to notice the sounds around you. Take another deep breath and become aware of the subtle air flowing in and out of your nose. If your mind starts to wander, gently bring it back to the present moment. The journey is not just about reaching a destination but also about being mindful of each step, each breath, and each sensation along the way. Pay attention to the emotions that arise without judgment. This practice of mindful exploration nurtures self-awareness, cultivates a deep sense of connection to the world, and is a step forward on the path to love and conscious living.

# CHAPTER 5

# Evolving Through Relationships

---

*Listen to your heart. It knows all things*
*because it came from the Soul of the*
*World, and it will one day return there.*

—PAULO COELHO

Since my trips to Spain and the Dominican Republic, I've placed a greater emphasis on cultivating deeper bonds with those closest to me, focusing on building relationships rooted in trust and understanding. I've observed a noticeable shift in my ability to provide them with the support they need, engaging with genuine curiosity and empathy.

As my mind is no longer clouded with survival instincts and the need to defend my point of view or identity, I find myself enjoying more peaceful and rewarding experiences that nurture my heart and soul.

Trusting has not been an easy process for me, which I believe is due to the unsafe conditions in which I grew up. I learned to protect myself from a very young age and, subconsciously, I brought this mindset to each of my relationships.

Let me take you back to a moment when I was living with my fiancé and my daughter, Val, who was still attending college.

Val exclaimed, "My mom doesn't trust anyone, not even me!" This response came when my fiancé complained about me covering up a password-protected Excel sheet containing login details. They both glanced at me as if they were sharing the world's funniest joke, yet it left me perplexed, trying to fully grasp the meaning of their reaction.

I never thought of myself as distrustful, and in that moment, I felt I was doing the right thing by not giving my fiancé access to every single password I had. However, my daughter's statement, coming from someone who knew me better than anyone else in the world, opened my eyes to a hard truth I had difficulty accepting. She acted as my mirror, revealing a clearer image of who I truly was even though it was challenging for me to see it.

## THE MIRROR OF RELATIONSHIPS

The quality of our interactions with others mirrors the relationship we hold with ourselves. Every exchange presents a chance for personal growth, whether through cultivating patience and empathy or learning to establish boundaries.

My lack of trust and self-compassion got in the way of building a nurturing relationship with my then-fiancé. I saw him through the lenses of someone I idealized, and I was harsh with him when he made a mistake, which in turn also made him harsh on me when I made a mistake. Unknowingly, I fostered an environment where we mirrored what we both lacked.

Today, my perspective toward my ex-fiancé has shifted toward greater empathy. I've come to understand the ways in which I demotivated him, not just within the confines of our personal relationship but also in our joint business venture. My need for control hindered his creative expression, especially as I micromanaged our website and logo development. I constrained him by fixating on details like fonts, color schemes, and artwork. I preferred a more conservative style, whereas he favored vibrant colors and a more innovative approach.

Reflecting back, I recognize the importance of having entrusted him with complete ownership of the project. Rather than imposing my own preferences, I should have emphasized what truly excited me about his designs and appreciated his unique expression. I lost the opportunity to see the man I loved flourish and the birth of a vibrant logo that perhaps would have grown on me.

I learned countless lessons from my relationship with my ex-fiancé. We had a painful breakup that helped me see many parts of myself I never knew existed. What I once perceived as a flaw in my ex-fiancé, I now seek to cultivate in myself. His laid-back demeanor mirrored my own struggle with relaxation. I now have come to appreciate the importance of incorporating downtime, enhancing my well-being. It's interesting to note how I previously undervalued creativity and relaxation, being overly focused on work. Now, I am actively nurturing these qualities within myself.

With Keri, my web designer, I now allow her creative expression to surprise me. When she designed my coaching website with bright orange colors, I initially thought it was too much. However, I quickly grew to love it. If I had micromanaged the website design as I had done in the past, I wouldn't have enjoyed it as much as I do now. Keri has said to me a few times, "I wanted to push you a bit," and for that, I'm grateful. I'm grateful for letting go of my need to control everything and allowing life and people to surprise me with their beauty and wisdom.

Many of us often find ourselves disliking traits we have suppressed within ourselves while simultaneously desiring others to embody the qualities we possess. Interestingly, we also tend to compare ourselves with others, wishing to possess certain attributes they have.

It's crucial to observe these tendencies without casting judgment and to introspectively ask, "What can I learn from this? Is this a quality I admire and wish to develop within myself? Or is it a trait I have denied in myself that needs more conscious recognition? Should I be practicing more patience and acceptance, or is it time to establish firmer boundaries?" Addressing these questions shifts our perspective from one of judgment to curiosity, opening up avenues for growth and learning with every interaction we have.

We are indeed all mirrors to each other; we reflect to others what is inside us. Reflecting to others what is inside us consciously is the beauty of relationships—a journey of growth and evolution together. By recognizing our own strengths and qualities, we also learn to appreciate and cherish the strengths and gifts of others.

## TOLTEC WISDOM, A GUIDE FOR SELF-REALIZATION

The Toltec wisdom has resonated deeply with me in my quest to understand what it takes to love more deeply, hold space for another person without projecting my beliefs to them, and look inward with curiosity and compassion. Realizing we are all divine beings, but it's our individual upbringing and conditioning that lead to the sense of separation, has deeply resonated with me. I no longer see good versus bad people. I now realize we all give the love we have within us in the way we can, or react from our lack of love. This reaction is often an unconscious response to our own inner wounds, inadvertently causing pain to others.

In his book *The Mastery of Self: A Toltec Guide to Personal Freedom*, don Miguel Ruiz Jr. explores the profound practice of unconditional love as an art of self-mastery, rooted in Toltec wisdom. By recognizing, releasing, and forgiving the self-judgments that stem from our conditioning, we become capable of recognizing and forgiving others when they act from their own conditioning (Ruiz 2016).

Our social conditioning, known as domestication, often leads us to seek love that is conditional and comes with expectations. When I reflect on my lived experience, the personal stories of those who have confided in me in my coaching practice, and the Toltec wisdom teachings, I've come to understand that lack of unconditional love is one of the biggest inequalities that exist. As we become more aware of the wounds we carry from our upbringing and life experiences, we gain the awareness and necessary tools to understand our emotions and establish healthy boundaries rooted in love, not fear.

Through growth and evolution, as we strive to show our authentic selves to the world, we begin to see ourselves more clearly, allowing the reflection of others to bring light to any unresolved aspects within us.

## THE INNER WORK

I'm grateful for the inward journey I have been on in recent years. From being my worst critic to becoming an ally, I'm discovering a new way of relating to myself and the world around me.

As I learn to embrace my imperfect self and feel more comfortable letting others see me as I am, I am becoming less prone to react by projecting fears and insecurities onto others or trying hard to be perceived in a certain way.

And when those moments of fear arise and I feel reactive, coming back to a place of understanding for myself and others is becoming easier. I now have more resources and practices that help me find my center. I can now pause, take a break, observe what is underneath those thoughts or feelings, and proceed after a few mindful breaths.

In my journey to healing, I have attended a few satsang gatherings with Daniel Shai, a spiritual teacher of applied spirituality who focuses on the lived experience of union with the divine. Satsang is "a Sanskrit word that means 'gathering together for the Truth' or, more simply, 'being with the Truth'" (2024).

At one of these satsangs, Daniel posed a thought-provoking question: Is joy inherently good or bad? My immediate response was "Good!" However, he challenged my perspective by asking how one would feel if joy persisted while a loved one endured immense suffering, unable to share in their sadness. What impact does this have on the person in distress?

He then delved into the concept of anger. Is anger to be deemed good or bad? I thought anger was bad. Daniel continued, saying, "Anger can serve us positively if we don't externalize it. That is, rather than focusing on who to blame, we can instead listen to the message our anger brings with it: Maybe we are really angry because we didn't stand up for ourselves, we didn't set a boundary and honor ourselves, or we're too complacent in avoiding taking an empowered action we know will propel us in the direction of our authentic expression."

I have come to understand our emotions are these amazing gifts we have, and the more we develop our ability to feel them in the body, the more we come to understand them and the messages they hold. Our feelings are influenced by our emotions and our thoughts, and it is sometimes difficult for us to detangle the two and go into spirals of suffering.

One Buddhist saying is "Pain is inevitable, but suffering is optional" (Perry 2017). Sitting with my pain before leaving my corporate job was important for me because it gave me the strength to evaluate the life I was living and create a different reality for myself. During the painful moments of my life, I have learned and evolved the most. Through listening to those difficult emotions, I have found a path forward to be in a better place for myself.

A few practices have significantly aided me in connecting more deeply with my emotions, enhancing my mental health, and fostering actions based on love and compassion rather than fear.

**Journaling:** Being able to put my thoughts down on paper and get more intimate with my own thinking has brought me a lot of understanding of my emotions. Many times, I have been torn about a decision or in turmoil, and the mere act of expressing my feelings and reactions on paper helps me find answers.

**Meditation:** Realizing we are more than our thoughts is truly liberating! Numerous meditation methods exist, but I personally engage in Primordial Sound Meditation (PSM). This technique enhances self-awareness and promotes mental clarity. PSM involves using a unique Sanskrit mantra given to me by my meditation teacher. This mantra is kept private to maintain its sanctity, making it even more special. By not sharing or using the mantra outside of meditation, we prevent the mind from associating it with other things. For example, if I mentioned "apple," my mind could wander to various apple-related thoughts. I silently repeat the mantra and gently refocus on it whenever distractions arise, without judgment. This practice improves our ability to redirect our thoughts in daily life, preventing us from getting caught up in unhealthy rumination.

**Yoga:** The true meaning of yoga is union with the divine. Besides the postures usually associated with yoga, we can learn specific principles to live a life more in harmony with each other and our planet. I have amazing memories of practicing yoga with incredible people and in wonderful places. I have done restorative yoga in the Dominican Republic with Anyi, virtually with my younger sister in Colombia, in the breathtaking views of Hawaii's Big Island with Erica, and with my purple yoga mat at home. Every one of those practices was equally healing for my mind, body, and soul.

**Nature:** I love connecting with nature in my backyard, going hiking, and, when possible, taking a forest bath, also known as *shinrin-yoku, a* Japanese concept that encourages us to take in the forest through our senses. Nature and its wisdom are constantly teaching us when we are in tune with them.

**Ceremonial Grade Cacao:** This drink is a sacred beverage for heart-opening and fostering deep connections with others. Whether alone or at special gatherings with fellow spiritual seekers, the ritual is simple yet profound, and I cherish it.

**Music and Dancing:** Music has also enriched my self-care practices by not only listening but also dancing and singing along. When I dance salsa and merengue, it brings me back to my Latin roots and reminds me of my early twenties in

Colombia. Other times, I enjoy ecstatic dancing where I move freely to the rhythm of music as a form of meditation. Another way I enjoy music is by singing sacred songs, which fosters positive emotions and gives me a sense of peace. I become in tune with melodies that make me happy and touch my soul.

If none of these practices resonate with you, consider what truly connects you to your essence. What connects you to the roots of who you are? When are you most grounded and connected to your heart?

## INSIGHTS FROM CHOPRA RETREATS AND VEDIC WISDOM

Throughout the retreats and Chopra courses I attended in 2023, I found myself deeply inspired by numerous new ideas and insights into human nature. A particularly transformative teaching was the realization that we exist as multidimensional beings. In the eighth century, Adi Shankara, a pivotal figure in Vedic science and yoga philosophy, identified these existences across three dimensions, or layers, a concept that profoundly influenced my understanding.

Our **physical body** is made of matter and energy and encompasses an extended body, a personal body, and an energetic body. The extended body refers to our constant interaction with the environment, in each breath we take, and the people around us.

The **subtle body** is the mind, intellect, and ego. The mind refers to how we experience life in regard to the level of awareness we possess, which creates our reality. The intellect is our ideas, concepts, notions, beliefs, and discriminations based on our lived experiences. And the ego, or self-image, is the aspect of our being that identifies with possessions and titles and is concerned with how we are perceived.

The **causal body,** or field of pure potentiality, is the domain of the spirit, which can only be understood through one's own experience. The causal body is the *personal soul* that contains seeds of memory and desire, the *collective soul* in which we honor myths and archetypes, and the *universal domain*, which is our notion of God—the universal spirit, which is pure potentiality (Brady 2017).

Through Chopra courses, I also discovered the transformative power of intentions. Our true essence is reflected in our deepest desires and intentions. By understanding and consciously selecting them, we can manifest what truly matters to us.

These are the four Core Intentions for the Soul from the Chopra meditation I learned and the specific meaning I assign to them:

- **Joyful, energetic body:** well nurtured with food, sleep, movement, and a healthy environment.
- **Loving, compassionate heart:** creating a safe space for myself and others while maintaining healthy boundaries. Recognizing that everyone deserves love and respect and is striving to do their best with the knowledge they possess.

- **Reflective, alert mind:** in tune with my senses and present to what is, paying attention to the stories I tell myself. Reframing beliefs that no longer serve me.
- **Lightness of being:** peaceful with the past and accepting life as it is in each moment (Gabriel 2022).

As I navigate the journey to embrace all parts of my being, I commit to my intentions to show up more mindfully in the world. This increases my capacity to have more meaningful and intimate relationships with others. And in these intimate relationships, we grow the most and find true joy and purpose in life.

When our minds are free from the weight of self-judgment and our assumptions about others, we place ourselves in a position to truly listen to our heart's wisdom. By releasing our grip on expectations, both for our future and for the actions of those around us, we create space to fully appreciate the wonder of life as it reveals itself. In this state of mindful presence, we unlock the heart's qualities of love, intuition, and creativity for ourselves and others.

# Mindfulness Moment

Embrace the profound wisdom your relationships offer. Take a moment to visualize the faces of those you interact with every day. Reflect on a recent challenging encounter and consider how the frustrations you experienced might indicate areas within yourself requiring growth. Perhaps these encounters are an opportunity to improve your listening skills, be more present and thoughtful, or enhance your ability to set boundaries. Pause for a moment and consciously breathe, embracing the lessons and teachings of that encounter. Exhale, releasing any resentment or resistance. In the vast classroom of life, we are all both learners and teachers. Embrace this continuous cycle of learning and teaching, as it lies at the core of our interconnected existence.

# CHAPTER 6

# A Journey Toward Acceptance

---

*Our ability to reach unity in diversity
will be the beauty and
the test of our civilization.*

—MAHATMA GANDHI

In the 2016 US presidential election, many of us found it increasingly difficult to have constructive dialogues with those supporting the opposing political party. Many of the conversations I took part in revolved around trying to persuade each other about who the best or worst candidate was. Misinformation on the internet and social media clouded our ability to truly listen to understand each other, creating greater division among us. Many of us were not equipped to find common ground to better understand others' viewpoints and perspectives in that political landscape.

Listening is a learned skill. For most of my life, I had a deep desire to be right. I was wired to listen to respond and think about what I was going to say next before the other person even finished speaking. I was not listening to *understand*. This need to always be right caused me countless disagreements and conflicts in relationships, ultimately limiting my enjoyment of life.

The Global Emotions Report highlights a worldwide struggle with loneliness, describing it as a silent pandemic. According to Gallup, one in every five adults lacks a reliable support person (Gallup 2022). Despite being surrounded by people and engaging in significant community work for many years, my inability to accept and connect with those closest to me left me feeling isolated and lonely.

## REFLECTIONS ON MY JOURNEY WITH VEGANISM

In 2018, I started a vegan diet after attending a lecture with Neal Barnard, MD, in Providence, Rhode Island. I found it educational and decided to pursue it to adopt a healthier lifestyle. Since I was already vegetarian, it wasn't too difficult a challenge since it only required removing a few animal products from my diet. After a couple of years of following my diet, I started to feel an amazing respect for animals and felt proud of being vegan. Being vegan was religious to me. It took a lot of discipline and determination to coordinate meals, mostly while traveling.

While I was visiting family in Colombia, we went on our usual search for vegan-friendly meals, which proved quite challenging since we were in a small city and Colombian cuisine includes meat in almost every dish. On some occasions, we all sat at the table, ready to order, and I would decide at the last minute there was absolutely nothing I could eat after finding out all the ingredients of the dishes and worrying about possible cross contamination of meat or dairy.

One day, as I was eating my vegan-friendly meal and feeling happy about my choice, I looked around the table and noticed everyone else—my sister, her husband, and my mom—had huge portions of red meat on their plates—bigger than the plate could hold. It seemed to me that my mom had ordered the greasiest piece of meat she could find on the menu. I became judgmental, and I took it out on my mom, giving them a lecture on healthy eating. I thought I knew better. I was on a mission to make everyone else vegan.

My good intentions got in the way of a true connection. Despite having a deep desire to have my family eat healthier, my persistence in imposing my values got in the way of connecting with them in meaningful ways. I couldn't fully enjoy those special moments with my family because I was unable to respect their life choices and meet them where they were by choosing love and compassion over judgment.

Recognizing the rigidity and judgmental attitude I'd developed due to my vegan diet, I decided to discontinue it in the summer of 2022. Looking back, I understand it wasn't the vegan diet itself that cultivated my judgment toward others who didn't share my dietary choices; rather, veganism brought my inherent judgmental tendencies to the forefront, making them more apparent to myself and those closest to me.

I hold a deep respect and admiration for veganism, both as a means to heal our planet and as a way to extend greater compassion toward animals. I am also mindful of the many vegans who consciously avoid a divisive "us versus them" mindset. Should I decide to adopt a vegan lifestyle again in the future, I would hold a profound respect for the dietary choices of others.

## CATHEDRALS AND SPIRITUALITY

At eleven years old, I found myself cleaning the altar in the picturesque church attached to the group home building where I grew up. The church was a stunning Catholic sanctuary with a golden altar, small yet spacious enough to accommodate up to two hundred worshippers on a busy day. I remember feeling glad I wasn't tasked with cleaning the bell tower that day. Sweeping the dusty staircase that led toward the bell, which was a house of bats, was terrifying.

Thankfully, this time, I was inside the church, cleaning the altar meticulously as the nuns ordered, but I thought it was quite boring. Sandra, a girl my age, had a smile on her face. I sighed and told her, "I can't believe we are going to be here all week next week!" She looked at me surprised and said, "This is such a special time of the year for me and my family," and started talking about family traditions during Holy Week as she cleaned the altar with utmost devotion.

I didn't have such faith, nor did I have good memories of Holy Week up to that point. The previous year, I was Protestant because of my mother, and I was made to become a Catholic overnight once in the group home.

Although I had some good times with other young people on Sunday mornings at the evangelical church my mom attended, many other times, I sat alone on the back bench at the church while my mom prayed and cried all morning in front of the altar.

For a long time, I harbored some internal hesitance toward religion, primarily because I didn't experience it as a loving and caring invitation. Growing up, religion was always imposed on me. I did, however, always consider myself a spiritual person.

During my time in Spain, I deeply connected with my spirituality in ways I had never experienced before. The mystical moments I encountered had a profound and lasting impact on me, influencing how I interact with others and view the world today.

The most memorable experience was visiting La Sagrada Familia in Barcelona, a remarkable architectural tribute to Jesus Christ. As I explored the basilica, the tour guide brought each piece of artwork to life with vivid descriptions. The place was incredibly beautiful and mystical. Pausing at a balcony designed for orchestral performances, I closed my eyes and envisioned musicians skillfully playing their instruments. As I imagined them, heavenly tunes reached my ears through the headphones.

When I opened my eyes and observed fellow visitors from all over the world, I first connected with their peaceful faces, and then I connected with a profound sadness in each of them. It felt as if I could sense their lifetime pains. At that moment, I felt an inexplicable connection with all of them, experiencing a deep sense of unity.

During my time in Montserrat, my mystical experience centered on a sense of self-realization, a moment of inner arrival when I no longer felt the need to search externally. My realization was that I had found peace within myself.

Today, I find myself feeling a deeper connection with others in ways I hadn't imagined before. I no longer desire to be right or to impose my values or beliefs on others. Now, I prioritize listening and accepting others for who they are. I am driven to seek experiences and opportunities that unite us rather than separate us.

## CONSCIOUSNESS AND SPIRITUALITY

My meditation practice has been instrumental for me to connect deeper with myself. Meditation encourages us to look past our busy minds, prompting us to contemplate questions like "Who am I?" and "What is my purpose?" These questions are not ones we necessarily seek to answer but rather focus points to guide our understanding toward what truly matters. Who am I beyond my name, my upbringing, my career, and my beliefs? Exploring these questions brings us closer to our core essence, which is pure consciousness. Awareness is the process of consciousness recognizing itself.

In the spring of 2023, I had the pleasure of reconnecting with Jeff Deckman, the esteemed Stevie Silver Award winner for his book *Developing the Conscious Leadership Mindset for the 21st Century: Insight for Leading Change, Improving*

*Employee Engagement, and Achieving Extraordinary Results.* Our initial encounter dates back to 2007, during my tenure at a Rhode Island state agency, where he offered his expertise as a business consultant and adviser to our small business initiative.

Jeff generously shared his views on religion, spirituality, and consciousness and how he communicates his views with leaders. Below, I'm sharing some of his insightful takes on these topics.

"Consciousness is about love and is looking to expand itself. Consciousness desires to expand itself to create more love. The frustration comes from things blocking that from happening. Consciousness allows you to see the love out there, but you must be in tune with a specific frequency. If you are low-wired, you can't receive it. Your consciousness is ready to advance when you notice your thinking is making you sick; [it is a sign that] your soul is ready for the next class. When you're bored in the class you're in and getting agitated [and] anxious... the ego is driving your interactions. Rely on consciousness to give your next step."

Jeff continues. "You can't think your way to a higher level of consciousness; actually, thinking is a lower form of this. What we seek is spiritual healing to get to that which opens our hearts and quiets the mind. Consciousness is not competing with your religious beliefs, as religion leads you to become spiritual and spirituality leads you to consciousness."

My biggest takeaway from my conversation with Jeff is higher levels of consciousness come with our capacity to love and grow spiritually. The specific path you choose to grow spiritually—whether through your chosen religion or through acts of kindness—is not as important as ensuring it leads you to a path of love and unity, not separation and division.

For too long, I lived my life in separation and judgment, viewing the world as me versus them. It wasn't out of a desire to offend or inflict pain on others; rather, it stemmed from insecurities I wasn't fully aware of. By sharing my journey from judgment to acceptance, I hope more people will seek out experiences that promote unity rather than living in judgment and fear. If I had learned this earlier on, then I would have had healthier relationships and more fulfillment in my life.

Those of us who didn't have a loving and nurturing environment growing up struggle the most on this journey to accept ourselves and others. I believe the journey to a less polarized world starts with each of us embracing the totality of who we are, training our minds for a kinder internal dialogue, and opening our hearts to love and compassion toward ourselves and others. By doing so, we start to recognize the beauty and wisdom in everyone around us, creating safe environments where genuine connections thrive.

## Mindfulness Moment

Mindfulness empowers us to confront our biases and acknowledge our prejudices with compassion and acceptance. It guides us on a transformative journey of self-discovery, where we validate our emotions without judgment. Say the next statement out loud: "I honor my emotions, observing them without judgment. I choose love and compassion over fear and judgment in how I respond to myself and others." Embracing differences becomes an opportunity for growth and understanding rather than an obstacle. Together, let's celebrate our diverse experiences and foster healing for all.

# PART II

# BELONGING IN THE WORKPLACE

# CHAPTER 7

# We Need Love in the Workplace

---

*Love and compassion are necessities,
not luxuries. Without them,
humanity cannot survive.*

—DALAI LAMA

During my earlier years in my professional career as a newcomer to the United States, I had a deep desire to prove myself to my boss. One day, I decided to take the initiative to make a purchase request for her. I knew how busy she was at that moment, and the task we needed to complete was important and time-sensitive. I wanted to go out of my way to make her life a little easier by helping prepare the document.

I had never made a purchase request before, but I felt like I could do it. I reached out to the accounting team and requested all the necessary information and appropriate documents for this task and completed it to the best of my ability.

As I approached Shana with the completed document in my hand, I was about to tell her what I had been working on, but before I could finish my sentence, she grabbed it from me, frustrated, and said, "You do not have the authority to make a purchase request." With the document in hand, she tore it into small pieces and threw them in the trash. As the pieces fell, some made it into the trash can and others landed on the floor and on my feet. She stormed out of the office, and I picked up the pieces of paper across the floor while tears filled my eyes.

I felt devastated. All I wanted to do was position myself as a valuable resource to my boss, but I felt my actions had done the opposite. If I had had a healthier relationship with myself back then, I might have realized her reaction had more to do with her than with me. Instead, I internalized the event and felt a lot of guilt for not having asked her prior to doing the invoice for her.

Knowing what I know now, I believe Shana was also responding to her own inner struggles and challenges in managing her emotions. While I lack details about her story or pain, I am certain it obscured her perception of my good intentions. If she had inquired about my actions and explained the protocol going forward in a compassionate and respectful manner, we could have both enhanced our trust and collaboration significantly.

## THE NEED FOR HUMAN CONNECTION
## IN THE WORKPLACE

Are you among the lucky few who genuinely love their job and cherish the relationships formed at work? If so, you belong to a minority. According to Gallup research, almost 60 percent of individuals in today's society feel emotionally disconnected from their workplace (Gallup 2023).

In today's world, leaders have a crucial responsibility to lead with empathy, truly seeing and understanding their employees. This approach not only fosters their development but also guides them in aligning their tasks with their strengths and passions, enhancing their job satisfaction.

To effectively lead and nurture engaged and empowered individuals and teams, leaders must first cultivate self-love. I had the pleasure of speaking with Eric Pliner, an expert in workplace and leadership, and the author of the book *Difficult Decisions: How Leaders Make the Right Call with Insight, Integrity, and Empathy.*

When I asked Pliner about the role of self-love in his leadership approach and its impact on his success, he shared, "Ironically, many leaders are driven by a lack of self-love. The desire to prove our worth, validate our value, and believe we matter often pushes us to do more, achieve more, and constantly strive for more. However, the significance of self-love in attaining our full potential and making a profound impact in the world always becomes evident. My moments of greatest triumph have been when I have truly embraced self-love, and interestingly, these are not typically the moments fueled by my greatest ambition."

According to Pliner, the gap between leaders who prioritize profit, performance, and productivity and those who value impact, intimacy, and interconnectedness will continue to widen. Both approaches will coexist, offering us more choices in how we lead and who we choose to follow.

Eric Pliner's insights into leadership dynamics resonate deeply in understanding the culmination of events that lead to a phenomenon known as "quiet quitting." As highlighted in Gallup's State of the Global Workplace: 2023 Report, the staggering rate of disengaged employees has a considerable financial impact worldwide, reaching an astonishing $8.8 trillion (Gallup 2023).

Leaders set the example and have the most significant impact on culture. However, everyone in the organization actively contributes to shaping it. What is celebrated and what is not tolerated are the factors that ultimately define the culture. I've been in workplaces where leaders were allowed to be disrespectful to employees simply because they were high performers or well-connected. They failed to grasp the adverse effects this has on individuals and the organization's financial performance.

The field of diversity, equity, and inclusion (DEI) emerged from a deep desire for love and belonging and aims to create more inclusive organizations. However, when not properly implemented, it often leads to increased division among us. Drawing from my experiences and discussions with a diverse group of professionals, it's clear that many diversity initiatives fall short of their intended goals. I have personally heard a few colleagues say, "I don't need to be part of the diversity initiative; that's for people of color," not realizing the intent of such initiatives is to celebrate, leverage, and appreciate all of our differences.

Anyi Espinal, whom I visited in the Dominican Republic at the end of 2022, spent ten years delivering DEI training in the hospitality industry and coaching leaders on fostering inclusive cultures. She witnessed the commitment of many organizations and their leaders to this important work. However, she also experienced frustration with the slow progress in the field. While she was part of a supportive team that held space for her during both good and challenging days, the pace of advancement in social justice and equity issues within the industry and across the nation left her feeling restless.

In Anyi's own words, "The term 'diversity training' had become stigmatized in the workplace. Despite well-intentioned efforts, the politicized environment and personal biases prevented genuine connection and understanding." Even as a DEI community leader, Anyi experienced burnout and disengagement.

Recognizing that a DEI mindset alone is not enough, she adds, "I loved my job because it had purpose and aligned with my personal mission. However, the increasing emotional demand from external forces began to weigh heavily on my heart." Anyi felt despair for others due to events like the killing of unarmed Black individuals, the separation of immigrant families, and the divisive political climate. This made it difficult to function in environments where productivity was prioritized over inclusivity.

Anyi shared that even companies with dedicated DEI professionals and established inclusion programs face challenges in effectively addressing the emotional impact of external factors on their employees. "In my role as training developer, we received requests from companies to develop content that addressed the immediate needs of human resources. These requests became increasingly focused on how managers could support employees of color in coping with the emotional toll the influx of bad news was displaying on their employees. Among employees, these manifestations were evident through emails to HR expressing dissatisfaction with how matters involving individuals with different cultural ideals were handled. It was also noticeable through short tempers, visible attitude shifts among usually pleasant individuals, a lack of interest in work duties, increased absenteeism, gossip, and subtle pleas for help that often went unnoticed by leaders."

Motivated by the profound grief caused by unjust events across the US, Anyi decided to create Casa Bienestar, a retreat space in the mountains of Santo Domingo where I spent time meditating and healing. She returned to a simpler, more peaceful life with her family in her native land.

Other outstanding community leaders and DEI professionals like Anyi have faced similar challenges and frustrations. Their passion for their work is undeniable, yet they often suffer from burnout because, despite the existence of leaders and organizations that prioritize employee well-being and social responsibility, many still do not. This discrepancy leads to a growing divide within our society today.

Loving and caring for each other requires us to recognize that beneath our egos and personalities, we are all fundamentally the same. We all have a natural desire for connection and belonging. And when we love and care for others, this inner force nurtures us as well.

The good news is the workplace is in dire need of love! In January 2024, I had the pleasure of speaking with Chloé Valdary, a trailblazer in the realm of DEI and the visionary behind the Theory of Enchantment. Chloé advocates for deep self-exploration, empowering individuals to embrace their humanity and acknowledge their ability to respond from a place of love and connection.

During our conversation, I asked Chloé, "What is your experience going into corporate environments teaching love?" To which she responded, "More and more people are definitely attracted to it. And I think that's because other types of programs they have been exposed to do not center the language of love." Chloé expressed her excitement as more employees within organizations are hungry for love.

Chloé recognizes that many individuals draw a clear line between their professional and personal lives, holding the belief that the love and care reserved for family do not find a place in their work environment. She argues that considering the significant amount of time dedicated to work, finding love and fulfillment in one's career and workplace is crucial.

Another insightful interview I held was with Tim Hebert, a perennial entrepreneur, visionary, and author of *The Intentional Leader: How Inner Authority Can Unleash Strong*

*Leadership.* In our discussion, he emphasized the importance of self-acceptance and authenticity to build strong relationships. He believes the quality of our relationships and the connections we are able to build with others is what's most important in life.

Tim used the metaphor of a Matryoshka Russian doll, which contains dolls of decreasing sizes nested within one another, to describe human complexity. He explained, "Most people only see the outermost doll. They observe our actions, possessions, and the superficial aspects of our identity." He argued that to truly understand someone, we must get closer, and it requires bravery to reveal our true selves to others in order to forge deep and meaningful connections. He continued, saying, "Some people need a guru or a near-death experience to wake up to the realization that they are lacking self-love and therefore not able to showcase love in their work and relationships."

His statement deeply resonated with me because I, too, had to endure a difficult life experience to awaken to the yearning for deeper, more meaningful connections in my life.

I hope more leaders and workplaces today create healthier environments for meaningful connections to take place and for people to be able to bring their full selves to work and foster each other's growth. It goes beyond personal fulfillment; it's about creating a positive impact, enjoying our work, and nurturing caring relationships. However, Gallup's research presents a disheartening view, indicating that the majority of workplaces leave employees dissatisfied. This dissatisfaction not only harms personal well-being but also decreases productivity and profitability.

Now, more than ever, we need love in the workplace. This type of love is *a deep respect and commitment to the flourishing of others by engaging with them through curiosity, empathy, and a genuine concern for their well-being.*

Seeing the good in each other and understanding the impact past experiences have on how we engage with the world is crucial. These experiences shape our perspectives, how we interact with others, and the awareness we bring to each moment.

Adopting the belief that "everyone is doing the best they can" might be difficult at first, yet it proves to be transformative, cultivating inner peace and enhancing all of our relationships in and out of the workplace. It frees us from the unrealistic expectations we may hold on to each other, and it gives us an attitude of curiosity and empathy to support each of us in our journey.

Leaders should set the example and create environments that foster compassion and understanding where there is no room for judgment and negativity; where employees are in the right jobs, utilizing their strengths; and where they are challenged with clear expectations and feel empowered to have honest conversations and negotiate with their leaders.

Love should encompass everyone in the workplace, serving as a unifying force that fosters sustainable growth and longevity for both leaders and employees. I hope love will have a profound impact on the business landscape, rippling out into the world. A foundation rooted in love should inspire organizations to recognize the significance of diversity and inclusion, both in practice and intent, nurturing an environment where everyone feels a sense of belonging and thrives.

I deeply value leaders who acknowledge and embrace the unique aspects of my identity and how my upbringing shapes my everyday experiences, but their genuine love and care are what have created an environment where I truly feel valued and flourish. Equally important is the understanding that the love we cultivate within ourselves extends to an abundance of love for others.

# Mindfulness Moment

To foster love in the workplace, each of us must cultivate self-love and mindfulness, which entails being fully aware of our emotional state. Take a moment to reflect: How can I connect with my emotions and listen to the wisdom they offer?

Our emotions serve as a guide, directing us toward what feels right and what causes discomfort, enabling us to advocate for ourselves effectively. By acknowledging and understanding our emotions, we can uncover underlying reasons for our unhappiness and consciously work toward creating a more compassionate and heart-centered work environment. Treating ourselves with kindness and empathy allows us to extend that love to others, fostering a culture where everyone feels respected and valued.

# CHAPTER 8

# Leaders Who Left a Mark

—

*Becoming a leader is synonymous with becoming yourself. It is precisely that simple, and it is also that difficult.*

—WARREN G. BENNIS

Since my first job at the age of seventeen, I discovered a deep affinity for work, which subsequently provided me with a sense of independence and self-worth. Throughout my career, the various leaders and managers I've had the privilege to work under have impacted me in profound ways, serving as role models and significantly shaping my personal and professional ethos. This chapter honors some of those leaders.

I've experienced a wide spectrum of leadership styles. While some leaders unintentionally rekindled childhood wounds within me, others spotted my potential and relentlessly encouraged me to become the best version of myself. I admired those leaders who empowered me, although oftentimes, I idealized them and felt disappointed when they fell short. Reflecting now, I see acknowledging my mistakes and imperfections was my own struggle.

Since I did not have family around, my career became the most important aspect of my life, and work relationships had a high regard in developing my self-esteem. I've often wondered if previous managers recognized the impact they had on my journey and whether they took pride in the fact I was devoted to my job and responsibilities. I always felt I had something to prove to every manager I had, and whenever a leader took notice of my work ethic by providing constructive feedback in a caring and respectful way, it motivated me.

## LEADERS WHO CARED

In 2006, only four years after I moved to the United States, I found myself extremely nervous when I realized I made a mistake on an insurance policy I sold. I imagined all the possible outcomes, and all of them ended with me being fired. The following morning, I pushed myself to work, knowing my boss would be in the office and would talk to me about it.

When he approached me, he didn't look angry at all. I was confused. He sat next to me and asked, "What did you learn from what happened yesterday?" I was relieved and proceeded to tell him my initial thoughts on the process and why I had done it the way I did. He seemed glad I could reflect on it and told me about some of the biggest mistakes he made earlier in his career. He created a safe space for me, so I felt heard and seen by him, and he didn't define me by what I did wrong but rather by my ability to reflect and learn from my mistakes.

My prior experiences when making a mistake were quite different. Raúl Méndez was a great man but a difficult boss. Many of us at Raulett, the company Méndez founded, feared his short temper. Raúl instilled in me a passion for perfectionism, which was the slogan for his company. While it served me well, it also brought me pain on numerous occasions. He was a leader who left a mark, both good and bad.

During my seven years at Raulett, I worked my way up to become an assistant designer, working directly under his direction—an honor with great responsibilities. Raúl, the designer and owner of the company, would discuss with me his vision of the garment and began to trace the most complex parts of the main design. Then I was responsible for completing the pattern, cutting the garment, and supervising its construction until it became the official sample. My responsibilities also included scaling the initial pattern for various sizes and sending them off to production. Any mistake in my work could affect hundreds of units in the manufacturing process.

Even though I was very cautious about my part of the process, a couple of times, something went wrong. I still remember the pain of being on the receiving end of both his disappointment and temper. He would raise his voice so everyone could hear him, and it was customary for the receiver to remain silent rather than debate his opinion. However, at the time, we tolerated his bad temper because he showed us he cared for us in many other ways. Despite his temper, Raulett was one of the clothing companies in the small region where I lived that cared the most for its employees.

Raúl always included us in celebrations of his successes and was generous when the company did well financially. Raúl was also a visionary and had extraordinary plans for all of us. He dreamed of building a manufacturing plant with a gated housing complex for the employees. It may not sound all that lofty to everyone, but the majority of us came from low-income communities, and this would have been a life-changing opportunity.

Unfortunately, Raúl died before we could see his dream come true. Leaders don't need to be perfect, but they should genuinely care about their people. Raúl not only showed genuine interest in all of us at the company, but he also created opportunities for many of us to grow personally and professionally.

In his book *Love Leadership: The New Way to Lead in a Fear-Based World*, John Hope Bryant, founder, chairman, and CEO of Operation HOPE, reflects on his early career and emphasizes the importance of authentic leadership and genuine care for others. According to Bryant (2009, 04:47:00), people are more forgiving of leadership mistakes when they believe the leader truly cares about them.

I recently connected with Lucy, one of my former colleagues at the factory. She said the following about Raúl Méndez: "A very good man with a noble heart hidden in an iron shell."

I don't know when Raúl built the iron shell or what was underneath his bad temper. All I know is he saw me, a young low-income woman with an immense desire to succeed, and gave me a chance.

After a change in leadership in one of my roles, I approached my new boss ready to notify her of my plans for the week and the ideas I had to further support merchants in South Providence. Katharine listened attentively and said, "Claudia, you are the expert in the community you are working with. Put a proposal together of how you want to do it, and let me know how I can support you." This interaction was quite different from the interactions I had had with my previous manager, where I didn't have as much autonomy to do the work or decide what projects to undertake by myself.

Katharine was always approachable, which made it easy to talk to her about any topic or ask her any questions. I didn't realize this back then, but she created a safe environment for me to be myself, which allowed me to do my job much better. I became more proactive in taking the initiative and coming up with innovative approaches to building bridges in the community. Katherine perhaps had a better relationship with herself, which allowed others to be themselves as well.

Jana was another leader who supported my career progression and professional development. Under her leadership, I became the first community development manager the bank had ever had. Jana empowered me to create and execute a comprehensive community outreach and educational plan for low-income communities across the bank's region.

I thrived in that role. Not only was I able to make a positive impact on people's lives, but I was given the independence to engage in community initiatives that held the greatest significance to me. Jana valued my opinion and trusted my ability to do the job. As she allowed me the autonomy to work, I gained confidence in my role.

Many leaders may underestimate their impact on people, especially on those from marginalized communities, who may hold unspoken fears like I once did. This fear isn't always obvious but may manifest as vulnerability to work stress and is worsened by a lack of support from leaders. When we are free from fear and fully valued, it serves as a strong motivator to do outstanding work.

I recently had a conversation with Anyi about a leader who had a profound impact on her life and career. She shared some poignant memories from her time at the Multicultural Foodservice & Hospitality Alliance (MFHA). The leaders she collaborated with there, along with the organization's culture and alignment with her values, not only propelled her professional growth but also facilitated her personal healing and allowed her to embrace her true self.

Working at MFHA offered a unique experience compared to her previous job, placing her at the forefront of the corporate world. It didn't take her long to recognize the significance of enhancing her skills to excel in her new role, specifically in English writing. She would often doubt her performance, double-check emails for spelling and sentence structure, and seek feedback from colleagues before sharing them publicly. She also became hyperaware of how leadership perceived her professional style—from her appearance to interactions with board members and industry leaders. Fortunately, the company president and vice president took a keen interest in empowering her language skills and implementing systems to support her best work.

In Anyi's words: "Both Gerry, the company president, and Andre, the vice president of operations, who was my direct supervisor, would encourage me to speak up in meetings and share my thoughts without fear. Although English was not my first language, there would often be a pause in my responses as I translated some words from my native tongue and then articulated them in English. However, they would simply wait patiently for me to express myself and often mentioned my thoughts were always worth the pause it took to hear them. Both of them were intentional in connecting me with mentors who would help me advance professionally and researched technical support to ensure my written communication became flawless."

Even though Anyi's English was often corrected during her early days on the job, she always felt the corrections were made in a supportive and nonjudgmental manner. She felt as if she had English teachers at work who recognized her potential beyond language barriers. This empowerment fueled her drive for excellence, as she knew she had leaders who genuinely cared for her and believed her future would be bright with the company and beyond.

Anyi felt a sense of appreciation and value as a whole person, not just as an employee. She further expressed to me, "Working with Gerry always felt like a privilege all on its own.

He would take time from his busy schedule to have lunch with me in my Latino neighborhood and ask me questions such as 'How are you feeling about where the organization is headed?' 'Where do you want to add value?' 'What program or approach is energizing you today?' and 'What should I do differently?' I cherished these conversations because my voice became more assertive, and transparent, and I mattered in the company."

Anyi cherished another memory when Gerry invited her on stage to share her inspiring "hair story." The moment was a courageous one when she decided to embrace her natural beauty and cut off all her chemically treated straight hair. In her own words, "It marked the beginning of a journey to self-love, one curl at a time. As I transformed my long hair into an almost bald style, I felt empowered like never before. It taught me to proudly showcase my true roots without any apologies. Being encouraged by my leaders to wear my hair in an afro, especially when seen by other Black women, who, like me, were taught that afros and curly, voluminous hair were deemed unprofessional and unhygienic, meant I was dismantling stereotypes, misinformation, and reinforcing the value of showcasing the full me."

As a leader, how are you caring for your people, and how are you helping them increase their self-love?

## SUPPORTING OUR PROFESSIONAL GROWTH

For myself and other female immigrants I know, work can become a home away from home. Work is where we put all of our aspirations and commitment. Many immigrants with little to no family in the country will spend most of their time working, oftentimes more than one job.

Immense pressure, uncertainty, and fear are present when migrating to a new country to either advance their studies, contribute to their families back in their home country, or become resilient in a new environment. This fear of failure adds a level of strain on the mental capacity of immigrants that others may not face.

Beyond adjusting to cultural differences and potentially learning a new language, immigrants are building a home and may not have support systems in place. A leader can help foster a safe space and supportive environment by getting to know them well and adapting to each individual's needs. Leaders may ask, "What existing support do you currently have or lack, either nearby or back in your home country?" or "What kinds of experiences have you witnessed in work environments and leadership?"

Compassionate leaders are making an effort to comprehend, embodying Simon Sinek's principle of "speaking last." When we feel acknowledged and understood, we feel secure and primed to give our optimum performance.

In my cultural context, the mentality that the boss is always right and employees should turn to their boss for all answers is ingrained, leaving little room for collaboration or influence in decision-making.

While not all immigrants may connect with the inner struggles I encountered, they face numerous challenges adapting to a new culture in a foreign land. Having a mentor who can help them navigate the workplace as they progress in their careers can have a profound impact on the rest of their lives.

A common trait of exceptional leaders is they seem to have a strong relationship with themselves and deeply value their people. By enhancing our self-awareness and self-compassion, we can also evolve into the compassionate leaders the world needs.

Leadership is not about perfection but authenticity, driven by a genuine care for one's team. Leadership is about fostering an atmosphere that nurtures growth and innovation, prioritizing psychological safety. Great leaders actively listen, understand, and then respond. When employees feel acknowledged, valued, and safe, they become fully engaged and strive for excellence. Balancing leadership and collaboration, leading with love, not fear, is vital to create a supportive environment that harmonizes personal growth and professional advancement.

# Mindfulness Moment

On our journey toward conscious living, regularly engaging in mindful reflections is crucial. Take a moment to contemplate the profound impact leaders have had on your life. Reflect on a leader who, whether consciously or unconsciously, may have let you down. What lessons did that experience teach you? Did it cultivate resilience, patience, or compassion within you? Now, consider a leader who nurtured your growth and development. What qualities did you most admire about them? As you uncover the lessons learned, you come to realize the qualities you admire in them already reside within you and are reflections of the leader you aspire to be.

# CHAPTER 9

# Longing to Belong

---

*Because true belonging only happens when
we present our authentic, imperfect selves to
the world, our sense of belonging can never be
greater than our level of self-acceptance.*

—BRENÉ BROWN

For a long time, I took pride in blending in and assimilating into the workplace, to the point where I lost my sense of self in the process. I have learned advocating for ourselves, honoring our values, establishing boundaries, and guiding others on how we want to be treated is crucial. Doing these things is how we bring the most value to teams, organizations, communities, and personal relationships.

In her book *Braving the Wilderness: The Quest for True Belonging and the Courage to Stand Alone*, Brené Brown delves into her journey to find a sense of belonging. She shares how, by accepting herself and embracing her personal narrative, she discovered how to truly belong to herself (Brown 2017, 04:12:00).

Throughout my career, I've been part of several organizations that created environments where I felt comfortable being myself and contributing. I want to highlight some of those cultures that nurtured my ability to express myself authentically.

One of these organizations was the International Institute of Rhode Island, now known as Dorcas International, where I served as a board director from 2008 to 2017. This nonprofit aimed to overcome cultural, educational, economic, and linguistic barriers, empowering individuals to achieve self-sufficiency and active participation in society.

Dorcas International cultivated a culture that celebrated diversity and was dedicated to supporting and honoring differences among all stakeholders. My perspective was unique and respected by the board, having been a beneficiary of the organization's services as a newcomer to the US, which made me feel like my voice held significance. Many times, I acted as a liaison during transitions, and I had the opportunity to participate in the search committee for the new executive director of the merged Dorcas International.

The leadership transition signified a major change with the retirement of director Bill Shuey, who held a special place in the hearts of everyone in the organization and the broader community. We followed a highly inclusive process to appoint Kathy Cloutier, who has proven to be an exceptional leader.

She spearheaded the integration efforts and prioritized a client-centered approach, especially in supporting immigrant families and low-income residents post-merger.

I credit the impact I had within the organization to the respect and support of my fellow board members, even during my early years when my English skills were still developing. Their openness to listen, ask clarifying questions, and understand my perspectives greatly boosted my confidence and capacity to actively participate in the discussions at hand.

In 2010, another organization where I felt a strong sense of belonging was Ascendus, where I was a business development manager for the Rhode Island region, the first dedicated person to the area in a few years. Their mission was to empower underbanked entrepreneurs by providing them with access to capital and financial education. What struck me most was not just the diverse mix of employees within the organization or the mission-driven nature of the nonprofit but also the culture of collaboration they fostered—a completely new and enriching experience for me.

During those first months, as I learned the financial education curricula and lending guidelines, team members from other regions would lend their time, expertise, and resources to support my training. While management did not mandate it, this value was shared and celebrated within the company. It fostered a sense of camaraderie and belonging among us, and we all felt proud to be part of the organization and support each other.

In 2011, because of my involvement in community work, I had the privilege of being anonymously nominated and ultimately selected to participate in the Leadership Rhode Island (LRI) Core Program. LRI's mission is to engage and connect people through shared experiences that positively transform individuals, organizations, and communities.

The LRI Core Program brought together a diverse mix of established and emerging leaders for an experiential community leadership program centered on statewide issues. This involved an overnight retreat, ten monthly daylong sessions, and a collaborative group project. At the retreat, the atmosphere was welcoming and informal, and no one wore fancy name tags with titles. The program attracted leaders from various industries and sectors, ranging from top corporate executives to nonprofit directors and community professionals like myself. It provided a unique opportunity for leaders from different fields to build strong connections.

My voice and perspective were appreciated and welcomed. I was unique in many ways among the over fifty leaders across the state. Our diversity of thought and experience is what secured us a seat in this program, and we embraced that, making it easier to be more open with each other.

This experience provided me with a greater sense of confidence and validation about the value I could deliver on a bigger platform. Up until then, I felt my value was limited to supporting marginalized communities. However, this experience helped me realize the interdependence that could exist across these groups and the ability we have to help each other evolve and learn from one another. Engaging with a diverse range of professionals on a more personal level led me to understand our similarities far outweigh the differences that divide us.

Attending the LRI ETA II class stands out as one of the most enriching professional experiences I've ever had. I had many treasured memories, such as the unparalleled experience of being aboard a US Air Force cargo aircraft and going on a police ride-along during criminal justice month. I found the debrief sessions, which took place once a month, to be particularly insightful. They followed a day filled with lectures, seminars, and tours. During these debriefs, we shared our perspectives with the group, providing each participant with a chance to see things from different points of view. On several occasions, hearing someone else's feedback made me reconsider my own viewpoints. This led to moments of introspection regarding unconscious biases I may have had due to experiences I had encountered.

During one of the monthly sessions, we visited the inmates of both the male and female prisons and learned about the different programs offered for inmates to be both occupied and productive during their time there. I remember thinking they were going to be okay after they completed their sentence.

During the debrief, classmates discussed the real issues of discrimination these individuals would face upon release, something I wasn't fully aware of back then. I became more empathetic, not only because of my experience of touring the prison but also the insights of some classmates who were passionate about this issue and familiar with the challenges and barriers inmates would face in society.

LRI aimed to foster greater understanding through collective dialogue and collaboration, ensuring a psychologically safe space where individuals were celebrated for who they were and were empowered to speak up. To this day, I keep in touch with many of my ETA II classmates; we cherish our bond. Regardless of our graduation year, each of us who has participated in the program has always proclaimed it to be part of "The Best Class Ever."

Over the years, I've stayed connected with LRI's community and actively participated in various events and initiatives. In 2014, I took on the role of volunteer coach for the Make Rhode Island Stronger initiative. This was a multiyear effort, undertaken in partnership with Gallup, aimed at significantly enhancing employee engagement in Rhode Island by implementing strengths-based training and education.

Being part of LRI's Strengths Coaches cohort was an amazing experience. I felt proud to contribute to work with such a significant impact and greatly benefited from the strengths-based culture we cocreated. This culture emphasized appreciating each individual's inherent talents, and it was a building block as I began to recognize and embrace parts of myself I had previously overlooked.

During my volunteer coaching role with LRI, I was afforded numerous opportunities for learning and growth. A particularly memorable experience was in January 2017, when I was provided the opportunity to facilitate a Strengths session for the Cabinet team at Rhode Island College (RIC). This event held special significance because it represented a full-circle moment as it was through my education at RIC I secured my first professional position in the US.

My journey as a volunteer coach ignited my passion to obtain my Gallup Strengths certification and empowered me to establish InnateFive, my own consulting firm.

You might wonder, what exactly is this strengths-based tool? And how does it impact individuals, teams, and organizations? At the heart of it, this approach enhances self-awareness. It helps individuals recognize their natural inclinations and the unique lens through which they view the world—their innate talents. Additionally, it sheds light on potential tendencies that could hinder their success or get in the way of the success of others.

When I completed the CliftonStrengths—the Gallup assessment I utilize in my work—I gained deeper insight into my talents and realized they could sometimes backfire when I was unaware of them. For example, due to my drive to constantly improve, my "Maximizer" talent might cause unnecessary tension with others if perceived as perfectionism. Discovering our innate talents is a powerful way to help us understand ourselves on a deeper level.

Discovering my daughter's top CliftonStrengths theme was "Competition" was an eye-opening experience. I had always advised her against comparing herself with others, not realizing I was inadvertently demotivating her. Val thrives on competition; she is driven by a desire to win and finds motivation in outperforming her peers. This competitive spirit, which I lack and mistakenly viewed as a weakness, is actually her strength. Learning to appreciate and support her competitive nature has allowed me to see her flourish in numerous projects and activities, fully embracing and utilizing her talents.

I now find fulfillment in helping teams foster environments of inclusivity where every individual is celebrated and valued for who they are. We embrace each person's unique path to self-discovery and self-acceptance, understanding we are all at the perfect point in our personal growth. Our mission is to interact with curiosity, empathy, and respect, with the goal of bringing out the best in each other. This philosophy nurtures a profound sense of belonging, both within oneself and among peers.

To cultivate a strengths-based culture, prioritizing the continuous development of each individual's potential is essential. This means engaging in regular, constructive conversations about employees' talents and passions. Organizations that focus on strengths employ more effective workforce development strategies. They emphasize the importance of meaningful work, leverage individual strengths, and foster authentic connections. In such environments, employees feel appreciated and supported not just in their professional roles but as whole individuals, thereby boosting the overall performance of the organization (2024).

Embracing our authentic selves is our greatest gift to the world. We must learn to embrace our narratives, not allowing them to define us but instead using them to enrich our understanding of who we are. We should wear our life's scars with pride, acknowledging the lessons they impart and fostering curiosity about the paths others have taken. Today, I confidently affirm "I belong to myself." This self-acceptance enables me to belong to more places than ever before.

# Mindfulness Moment

On the journey to accepting our true selves, recognizing and embracing our past is essential. Accepting ourselves is about taking pride in our origins, understanding their role in molding us, and acknowledging that we always act according to our current level of awareness. Reflect on a moment when you felt truly alive and when you were proud of yourself, and the positive impact of your actions. What made that moment stand out? How can you create more of those moments in your life? As you inhale, cherish a sense of gratitude for your being; as you exhale, let go of any negativity in the way of your authentic expression. By making peace with our past, we embark on a transformative journey of self-acceptance and a deep sense of belonging.

# PART III

# A PATH TO HEALING IN THE WORKPLACE

# CHAPTER 10

# Mindfulness: A Path to Well-Being

_What happens
when people open their hearts?
They get better._

—HARUKI MURAKAMI

After leaving my corporate job, I began experiencing stress in my own business. Although I love facilitating workshops and coaching sessions to help others embrace their strengths, handling administrative tasks, worrying about uncertainties of the future, seeking clients, and sending proposals without responses felt overwhelming.

To address this, I hired Damian, a mindfulness coach, for guidance. Just a few coaching sessions with him proved to be transformative. The tools he shared have become invaluable in managing stress. One day, I accidentally closed a detailed invoice I had been working on without saving it. I felt frustrated, but recalling the mindfulness advice "Stop, take a breath, observe, and proceed," I paused, gazed away from the screen, took a deep breath, and observed what sensations, thoughts, or emotions were present without needing to change or judge them. I regained composure almost immediately, and with a clear mind, I proceeded to redo the invoice, amazed at how easy recalling all the details without needing to check my calendar or files was.

Clarity and ease emerge when we handle tasks without allowing ourselves to be overwhelmed by stress. Pausing when stressed and being present is a practice I commit to, not a skill that is second nature. For those who also don't possess these traits innately, I encourage cultivating compassion and understanding either for yourself or for those around you who have not yet developed them.

I noticed a significant shift in how I handled stress during a work trip last year. I was hired to facilitate a team-building workshop for a client in Iowa and planned to fly out early morning on Sunday to ensure I could deliver the workshop on Monday. Although I managed to board my flight on time, we were delayed on the tarmac for over two hours before being told to deplane. Weather-related delays affecting other flights had caused a ripple of disruption, leading to chaos at the airport.

Knowing I needed to reach Iowa on time, I tried to find an alternative route. Initially, it appeared a nearly impossible task, as the earliest flights to Iowa were scheduled for Tuesday—an unacceptable delay, especially since I had thirty-nine people attending my Monday workshop. However, I remained calm, focusing on my breathing and staying mindful of the unfolding situation. I observed exhausted families, frustrated passengers, and worn-out customer service representatives grappling with long hours and endless queues of aggrieved customers.

In my interactions with the travel agency, I tried to empathize with the person on the other end of the line, politely requesting any assistance they could offer. To my surprise, they found a first-class ticket on a flight that, while not taking me to my exact destination, would get me close enough to rent a car and drive the remaining distance.

Consequently, I landed in Minneapolis, Minnesota, on Monday morning and enjoyed driving through the cornfields to Dubuque, Iowa, to deliver the workshop that same afternoon. Despite feeling utterly exhausted by Monday evening, I was elated I had not let my client down or disappointed those who had traveled to participate in the workshop.

In the midst of chaos, I found the empathy to connect with others, experienced my first-ever first-class flight, and felt like a superhero. Previously, I would have been consumed by my own stress without considering those in more difficult situations, like the travelers I encounter with small toddlers. Life's journey doesn't always go smoothly or as planned, but we can always choose to respond in more mindful and compassionate ways toward those around us. I was proud of maintaining this ethos throughout my challenging travel experience.

## THE IMPACT OF STRESS ON INDIVIDUALS AND BUSINESSES

Some of the most stressful experiences I faced at work were associated with sales roles, even when selling event tickets through the nonprofit work I was involved in. Selling caused me significant anxiety, as I did not enjoy asking people for money and had to focus on fulfilling sales quotas rather than servicing my clients. However, when I was in roles where I could focus on serving others, stress took on a different significance—becoming a driving force. I thrived under pressure in those situations, making stress a regular part of my life. However, as a result, I had less time for my loved ones, and it negatively impacted my personal relationships.

I experienced the highest levels of stress when working under certain managers I didn't feel comfortable approaching with questions or seeking help when I felt stuck. In those moments, stress affected me the most, significantly impacting my well-being and mental health.

Being overwhelmed at work is not a unique experience. In today's fast-paced corporate world, burnout is a prevalent issue affecting both the physical and mental health of employees and, consequently, the bottom line of organizations. I realized my stress stemmed from three factors: first, my desire to overachieve; second, a mismatch between my talents and passions; and third, inadequate support from certain managers. Unfortunately, for others, stress may stem from toxic work environments that neglect employee well-being altogether.

According to Gallup's report, *Employee Burnout: Causes and Cures*, 76 percent of employees experience burnout at least sometimes, and 28 percent are burned out "very often" or "always" at work. While the number of hours worked plays a factor in burnout, the highest correlation to someone feeling burned out at work is significantly influenced by manager behavior. According to the study, the top five factors are unfair treatment at work, unmanageable workload, unclear communication from managers, lack of manager support, and unreasonable time pressure. Although managers hold this immense responsibility, oftentimes, they are not equipped with the necessary training and support to be great leaders. Through no fault of their own, this will cause burnout for the managers and can easily cascade through the entire organizational structure (Wigert and Sangeeta 2018).

Last year, I had the opportunity to interview Liam, who shared his firsthand experience with the significant ripple effects of stress and burnout. Liam worked at an investment bank within a fast-paced industry group that had been undergoing substantial changes in the past few years. Within his first nine months in the role, the team faced considerable attrition, forcing Liam and a few of his peers to quickly adapt and take on additional responsibilities, including covering clients and handling deals that would typically be assigned to senior analysts or associates.

Liam began feeling burned out as the work hours increased and the team was unable to fill the vacancies quickly enough. As months passed, more work piled on with the added responsibilities of training new hires, which created more stress and more hours. Liam explained, "It wasn't just the junior staff. Our managers were overworked, and it was a regular occurrence to see most of the team online until late hours." He noted that although his managers were trying their best to control the situation, many regulatory and internal changes were happening simultaneously, which were out of their control and affecting everyone.

While the hours were exhausting, Liam said the most stressful part was the overwhelming workload expected to be completed under tight deadlines and what felt like a false sense of urgency for some tasks. This led to many all-nighters for some projects that ultimately wouldn't make it through or deliverables that wouldn't be reviewed for weeks or sometimes months.

Liam found himself increasingly frustrated by the lack of clear guidance from upper management and the frequent changes in priorities. He acknowledged that this was a result of unclear communication and decisions made at higher levels of the hierarchy. Nonetheless, conversations with senior leaders on the team would often end with "It is what it is" in a defeated tone. Liam observed a pervasive feeling of hopelessness among everyone, who, without much complaining, would just carry on with their tasks. He witnessed leaders at all levels—from staffers to managing directors—working during weekends and vacations, unable to disconnect from work. The pressure and stress originating from senior leaders affected multiple levels of management, extending down to the most junior analysts.

During our discussion, Liam expressed how the absence of work-life balance and chronic stress had adverse effects on every facet of his life, impacting his mental and physical health, as well as his family and social life. Despite pushing himself to excel in that environment, he chose to pivot his career to prioritize his overall health and wellness after two and a half years in the role.

Gallup identifies five key areas fundamental to a person's well-being: career, social, financial, physical, and community. Surprisingly, it was found that the most important was career, having the strongest impact on an individual's overall well-being. Those with a high career well-being were more than twice as likely to be thriving in their life overall (Pendell 2022).

In addition to its negative effects on the individual, productivity, and business results, the total economic impact of stress on US employers was estimated at $300 billion, per an analysis conducted by the American Institute of Stress. The primary factors contributing to the economic impact were attributed to absenteeism, turnover, diminished productivity, increased medical costs, and increased legal costs (Kern 2022).

Leaders can guide individuals toward awakening their best selves, fostering a healthier and more productive work environment. They can promote mindfulness practices that help individuals stay present and find joy, purpose, and meaning in their work, and create safe spaces for genuine self-expression (Wigert and Sangeeta 2018).

When leaders don't prioritize their team's well-being, it detrimentally affects everyone involved. Mindfulness and self-care in both personal and professional realms can elevate levels of happiness and fulfillment. They nurture healthier relationships, enhance mental health, and amplify satisfaction in daily activities. These benefits underscore the fact that investing in wellness is not only a moral obligation but also a sound economic strategy.

## Mindfulness Moment

In today's multitasking world, dedicating ourselves entirely to a single task can be surprisingly rejuvenating. Choose an activity—it could be working on a project or something as simple as drinking a cup of tea—and commit to being fully present in that moment. Notice the sensations, the textures, the temperature, the colors, and any sounds associated with the task. If your mind starts to wander, gently guide it back to the activity at hand. This practice of monotasking not only enhances the quality of the work done but also reduces stress levels, allowing for a richer, more connected experience. We all have the capacity to interact with the world in ways that enhance our own well-being and allow us to be more present for those around us.

# CHAPTER 11

# The Healing Workplace: A Pathway to Flourishing People

---

*Business can be the most powerful
force for good in the world.*

—BOB CHAPMAN

During the last couple of days of my trip to Spain, Joan told me he wanted to give me a gift. We were at his home in Barcelona when he reached under the bed for a small box. As I looked at the box with curiosity, he opened it and took two books out, leaving many others in the box. And he asked, "Which one do you prefer?" I don't recall the title of the other book, but the one that caught my eye was *Sacred Commerce: Business as a Path to Awakening* by Matthew and Terces Engelhart.

This book was the perfect reading companion for my trip back to Providence. I was so amazed that there was such a business out there in the world. Coauthors Matthew and Terces Engelhart wrote the book to share the tools they learned in their own enterprises for building a spiritual community at the workplace.

While reading about how they fostered a spiritual community and culture of appreciation at Café Gratitude, I envisioned what it would be like to work in such an environment.

At Café Gratitude, employee well-being is central to their business ethos. They have developed various practices to foster a sense of presence and gratitude, including daily mindfulness sessions and gratitude circles where each member shares something they're thankful for. These practices create a positive, inclusive work environment and help employees cultivate positive mental habits that can improve their overall quality of life (Engelhart and Engelhart 2008).

In the spring of 2023, intrigued by Café Gratitude, I reached out to Terces and was fortunate enough to engage in a few virtual meetings with her. Our first meeting was profoundly special and intimate, making me feel deeply connected as if our paths had crossed long before, allowing me to openly discuss anything with her.

Terces radiated wisdom and love, and one of the most impactful statements she shared was, "Our work is removing any barriers that prevent us from connecting with the love that already exists within us." While I was familiar with this concept through the words of Rumi, one of my favorite poets, she helped me understand it at a deeper level. The essence of our being is love, something we deeply yearn for, yet we've been conditioned to guard ourselves to avoid pain. Thus, our task is to recognize and nurture this love within ourselves and in others, allowing us to forge relationships where love and light can flourish.

During another conversation I had with Terces, I shared with her my vision for this book and asked her, "How do you create an environment for employees to do their own inner work, feel cared for, and have somebody to hold space for them when they need to, yet remain productive and get things done?"

Below are some of the insights she shared with me:

> *Ultimately, a business won't adopt a transformation if it risks its existence because the business itself is what sustains it. Let me share a few things with you.*
>
> *So, the first insight is to create a sacred space, which is crucial. We achieved this by naming our dishes so that when employees looked at the POS system, they saw positive affirmations reflecting back at them. We make a conscious choice to remain grateful, regardless of our circumstances. Our overarching theme is centered around gratitude. You might choose a different theme that resonates with you, but for us, it's about instilling a sense of gratitude in people, no matter their situation.*

*Second, 'Be the space for all of it' means being present in one's own human experiences, as well as those of others. Every morning, employees share any obstacles preventing them from being fully present and receive support when needed. Third, 'Be in the game' means everything is an opportunity to grow, expand, and awaken. And the fourth insight is 'Be an invitation.' Consider that the only real invitation is 'Who I am is love, and I'm here to serve you.' So being an invitation is doing all of the deep work to get that you are an empty vessel through which love can flow.*

*You know, one of the things we say is 'If you want to accelerate performance then you lower tolerance.' If you become this person who just tolerates anything and everything, the bar of performance will drop.*

*Sometimes love is like, 'No, we actually don't do that.' In our case, no, you actually have to come to work with a clean uniform. You can't just turn it inside out. You actually have to show up with a clean uniform.*

*You want to create healthy boundaries that help people grow inside of whatever the culture is that you're presenting as a possibility for people.*

Terces felt proud that even individuals who only spent a few months working at Café Gratitude experienced personal growth. When she asked employees about the benefits of their tenure, responses such as "Oh my gosh, I never even

knew I had an internal dialogue until I worked for you"
were common.

Megan Marie Brien, the Vision Keeper for the Engelharts,
contributed the foreword to the book *Sacred Commerce*.
Within her narrative, she beautifully articulates the
profound influence her experiences with the Engelharts
had on her life. Here is an excerpt from her reflection:

> *I habitually doubted and judged myself, I constantly
> regretted things I did and said, and I was scared.
> I foresaw a future of being in and out of hospitals,
> paying for expensive treatments, and "fighting" illness.
> I felt stuck. I felt alienated and alone, experiencing
> arguments, break-ups, and disappointments over and
> over again. I was caught in my own suffering... Café
> Gratitude swept me off my feet. My training in the art
> of Sacred Commerce provided me the opportunity to
> transform myself into who I had always wanted to be.
> Now, I get to interact with the world in a way I feel
> proud of. Through my participation in this business,
> I love who I am and the work I do. I can authentically
> declare I am completely healed.*

For Megan, the process of transforming into someone she
was truly proud of wasn't easy. In the book's foreword,
she explained the initial discomfort she felt to be in an
environment encouraging her to look within and how, with
time, she managed to release anger and old wounds that no
longer served her to create a more fulfilling life for herself.

I wonder how different my life would have been if, instead of working for a food chain in 2002, I had worked for Café Gratitude. Discovering then that I had an internal dialogue, realizing I was more than my thoughts, and cultivating a healthier relationship with myself would have led to improvements in my relationships and how I engage with the world earlier on. I know it would have dramatically improved my life, but this book as it is would not have been written. Today, I'm grateful to share my story of inner struggles with the world so others don't have to endure them alone and they can know there is a better way to live our lives.

Imagine a world where leaders and workplaces prioritize the well-being of their employees above all. Environments rich in resources, guidance, and coaching could empower employees to forge deeper connections with themselves, their work, and their peers. Such a transformative approach has the potential to turn workplaces into spaces where individuals truly enjoy being.

In my research for this book, I discovered a vast array of resources, initiatives, movements, and organizations all aimed at enabling leaders to lead with empathy and understand the profound impact they can have on individuals, organizations, and society as a whole.

I want to acknowledge Martin E. P. Seligman for his extensive research into happiness and well-being in the workplace. His PERMA Model outlines the characteristics of thriving individuals through positive emotions, engagement, relationships, meaning, and accomplishments

(PERMA), providing a holistic view that touches on emotional, psychological, and social well-being. It aims to foster positivity, achievement, purpose, and social connections, granting us profound insights into pursuing a fulfilling life for each of us (Madeson 2017).

In December 2023, I had the privilege of meeting Thomas Eckschmidt, a renowned thought leader and business conscious strategist. As the cofounder and CEO of CBJ Conscious Business Journey, he leads a global network of certified consultants aimed at fostering a more conscious business ecosystem. Additionally, he coauthored *Conscious Capitalism Field Guide: Tools for Transforming Your Organization*, which provides practical tools and expert advice for integrating conscious leadership and practices into business operations.

During our conversation, Thomas shared valuable insights on various topics, including purpose, values, emotions, love, leadership, and social change. His dedication to a purpose-driven career, guided by his values, was truly inspiring. Learning about the principles of conscious leadership and how they promote the well-being of all stakeholders by creating a culture of higher purpose, values, and compassion was fascinating. Furthermore, Thomas discussed his decade-long commitment to helping leaders evolve into better versions of themselves, leading with empathy and understanding.

Thomas illustrated his approach to working with conscious leaders worldwide by sharing a relatable airport story, saying, "Imagine you're at the airport. You approach the check-in desk, and the clerk informs you, 'Oh, Claudia, there's been a change with your flight.' Naturally, you might be hesitant to hear more. But, if instead, they said, 'Claudia, I have some exciting news. Your flight has been upgraded,' your reaction would be completely different. This demonstrates the power of our word choices. Initially, my goal was to accelerate the transformation of businesses. But I've come to realize it's not just about upgrading businesses but upgrading people. Hence, my focus now is on accelerating the evolution of leadership. Because when leaders improve, businesses improve."

My conversation with Thomas led me to reflect on the transformative impact of conscious leadership in business and beyond. I realized leaders who elevate their consciousness find greater peace in their decisions and experience the satisfaction of helping others reach their fullest potential.

The concept of conscious capitalism was introduced by John Mackey, cofounder of Whole Foods, and Raj Sisodia, a marketing professor, in their book *Conscious Capitalism: Liberating the Heroic Spirit of Business*.

Advocates like Mackey and Sisodia argue that businesses can fulfill a social responsibility by generating value for all stakeholders while embodying the principles of conscious capitalism. This philosophy suggests companies, exemplified by Southwest Airlines, Whole Foods Market, and The Container Store, operate with a purpose that transcends mere profit. Instead, profit is viewed as a means to fulfill a greater mission. Research indicates businesses following Conscious Capitalist principles tend to outperform those solely focused on profit, showcasing the long-term advantages of this mindful business philosophy (2024).

At the 2019 Conscious Capitalism Annual Conference, John Mackey stated, "I have learned how to use my own sense of purpose and passion to help others find their own sense of purpose, to acknowledge and appreciate the team for their efforts, and to do something that is personally liberating for me, which is to lead with love." Mackey understands the profound liberation that comes from filling his heart with love and leading from such a place. He also recognizes that love propels us further, both in business and as a society.

In a Forbes article entitled, "Why Conscious Businesses Will Lead the Next Paradigm Shifts," Keda Edwards Pierre highlights how conscious businesses pave innovative paths that may not be immediately clear. Embracing change, though daunting, is crucial for fostering innovation and progress (2021). As we learn how to lead with love, give utmost respect to others, and commit to their flourishing, we create businesses not only resilient to adversity but that thrive in times of change.

So the time is now for more companies to embrace business as a path to awakening to a better way to live and work. During our discussion, Jeff Deckman described himself as a "healer of organizations." Jeff advocates for a self-aware, introspective, and empathetic leadership style that carefully assesses the impact on all stakeholders. His innovative approach to organizational dynamics views organizations as living, breathing organisms rather than mechanical systems.

In Jeff's words, "Organizations are organisms. So the challenge is, how do you blend this need to see the human and to work with the collective genius? How do I mobilize that? Put it through a form, not a structure, but give it form so it can think, it can breathe, it can move, it can contribute, it can fight, it can heal... and I can allow for that, but at the same time, there's accountability, there are measurements, and there's performance... Now you've created an organization that's high-performing and self-rejuvenating." This remarkable perspective blends a higher level of consciousness with sound business practices, humanizing operations to improve productivity and prevent burnout.

As a leader, Jeff also acknowledges the importance of creating heart-centered cultures with freedom for people to be who they are and evolve together. He says, "We can't manage others or give people coaching when we're angry with them. But when you love your colleague, your anger can turn into empathy. To love a colleague may require you to connect to the why and the how they are where they are. And, you may not need to know exactly how they were raised or all the challenges they may be facing. But I hope, as a conscious leader operating from love, you can manage your own emotions and show others empathy and compassion. If the person meets you short of the love you provide, you still give them love, support, and empathy. And if you were not able to move the needle forward for the person, organization, or team you want to impact, know you may not be the teacher they need at this time. Provide some outlets for them to explore and move forward without remorse."

Another leader who puts his people front and center is Bob Chapman, the CEO of the prominent industrial equipment manufacturer Barry-Wehmiller Companies, which boasts a workforce of over ten thousand employees and is dedicated to guiding his company with a philosophy he terms "truly human leadership." He measures success by how the company impacts people. Chapman underscores that every employee is "somebody's precious child," deserving of care and respect. He champions leaders who genuinely care for others, stating this as the essence of true leadership (2016).

In a TEDx Talk, Mr. Chapman shares a story about Steve, one of the employees who came to a management meeting to be recognized for his work. After a discussion about numbers, performance, and profits, Mr. Chapman asked Steve, "How did it affect your life?" to which Steve responded, "I'm talking to my wife more... Since we embraced this people-centered leadership... I have a chance to contribute my gifts... I go home feeling valued... And when I go home feeling better about myself, I find I'm nicer to my wife... And when I am nicer to my wife, she talks to me." That day, Mr. Chapman decided he was going to measure the reduction of the divorce rate among his employees (2012).

When we align our work with our personal growth and awakening journey, we redefine success to encompass joy, meaning, and connectedness. Adopting this empathetic approach in the workplace leads to a more productive and innovative organization and also nurtures healthier, happier individuals who positively impact their families and the wider society. By embracing this new paradigm, we realize that, indeed, "Love Is the Path."

# Mindfulness Moment

Practicing mindfulness has the transformative power to cocreate a nurturing and flourishing workplace. Take a moment to reflect on your colleagues, those with whom you interact most. Jot down their unique talents and the qualities you appreciate about them. Find meaningful ways to express your admiration. By openly and sincerely recognizing the value each person brings to the table, you foster love and respect, strengthening the bonds within your team. When we embrace gratitude, we respond rather than react, making heart-centered decisions. This simple shift in mindset cultivates an environment where every individual feels valued and engaged, empowering them to unleash their full potential.

# Conclusion

---

*When we deny our stories,*
*they define us.*
*When we own our stories,*
*we get to write a brave new ending.*

—BRENÉ BROWN

I find myself with a renewed sense of purpose as I write the last pages of this book. I feel hopeful that my personal story has shed light on the impact you can have on the lives of others.

I feel incredibly grateful for the journey that has led me here. Through confronting my inner struggles, I've come to cherish the peace I now experience and the quality of the relationships I have in my life today.

Embracing my true self instead of who I thought I should be has made me more aware of the world around me. Feeling like I am enough has been liberating; it freed my mind from defending my worth or proving myself. This new perspective allows me to be more present and genuinely interact with others, seeing them with curiosity and compassion.

My journey toward self-acceptance started with understanding and honoring my values. By reflecting on my past and how it shaped me, I made peace with it, seeing the struggles as gifts. This process of self-discovery heightened my awareness of my tendencies and triggers, and I learned to observe them without judgment.

Sometimes, our self-awareness grows through feedback from those who care enough to point out truths we might not see. A close person once told me, "Your need to control likely stems from the chaos you encountered in your childhood." Although unsettling at first, this insight was invaluable. It brought this aspect of myself into conscious awareness, giving me the power to choose differently.

As I acknowledge that life is challenging for all of us, I become more compassionate toward others, and I accept life as it unfolds. Releasing expectations opens my eyes to the beauty and wisdom present in everyone and everything.

Today, I feel grateful for everyone who has come into my life and the valuable lessons they have taught me. Each individual, whether briefly or for an extended period, has left an indelible mark on my life, shaping me into the person I am today.

I'm now blessed with incredible friends and soul sisters, and I'm experiencing the most rewarding relationship with my family. The profound connection I've forged with my daughter, sister, mother, and father is now my greatest source of joy.

My journey toward a more mindful life is just beginning. I acknowledge that I have so much growth ahead of me. However, I can continue my personal and spiritual growth while accepting who I am today, and that has been the biggest shift in my life.

In the most difficult moments of my life, I yearned for my leader to care about my well-being and nurture my potential instead of pointing out my shortcomings. I wanted to feel like I mattered as a person, not only as an employee. This sentiment echoed across concerning disengagement statistics, the increasing unhappiness globally, and in numerous discussions with colleagues, which made me realize my experience was far from unique.

I hope more organizations across the globe invest in their people and foster cultures of genuine curiosity and empathy. Leaders should be equipped with emotional intelligence skills to effectively nurture and empower each member of their team. When leaders can do this, employees will be able to bring their full selves to work.

I recognize my privileges and know not many people going through major life challenges and disengagement at work can leave their jobs and embark on experiences of self-discovery as I did. I acknowledge that for most people, these experiences may be out of reach due to financial constraints, having young children at home, or other responsibilities.

This presents an opportunity for workplaces to become sanctuaries for healing.

Today's leaders are navigating an ever-evolving landscape where an increasing emphasis is placed on creating workplace cultures that promote personal growth, job satisfaction, and a strong sense of community. Tapping into the full potential of each employee by aligning their strengths and passions with their roles is essential. Leaders can boost employee well-being and drive company success by nurturing inclusive environments, which value authenticity, creativity, and emotional intelligence, where everyone can flourish.

As we continue our journey of self-discovery and find beauty and wisdom in each other, the love and care we share will positively impact everything around us. Let us explore, with open hearts and conscious minds, and cocreate more fulfilling lives for all of us.

## Mindfulness Moment

Take a moment to reflect on your life's journey and recognize its significance. The love within you is a precious gift to share with others. Embrace it and celebrate it, letting it guide your path forward. Remember, self-love can always grow. Love is the path that reveals our inherent beauty and helps create the life we desire. Let's commit to being generous with our love, creating a more just and harmonious world for all.

# Acknowledgments

---

I am immensely grateful to the myriad of individuals whose incredible support has been instrumental in my book-writing journey.

To my soul sister, Anyi, for your love and the countless hours we spent working together on this project. Your belief in me and unconditional support have been beyond what I could have ever asked for.

To Val, your love and dedication played a pivotal role in my journey to the finish line. I sincerely couldn't have achieved this without your support.

A heartfelt thank you to Eric Koester and the exceptional team at Manuscripts LLC. I appreciate the steady support and thoughtful accommodations throughout the writing process. I extend my deepest gratitude to Angela Murray, John Palisano, Gina Champagne, Kristy Carter, Heather Romanowski, and Nadara Merrill. Each of you played a pivotal role, offering precisely what I needed and more throughout my writing journey!

I'm thankful to my wonderful neighbors, Erica and Bruce, who have been pillars of support during difficult times. Erica, thank you for your love and wise counsel.

Brett, my gratitude to you for teaching me how to love and hold space, and for believing in *Love Is the Path* right from the start.

I'm grateful to Mom and my sister Juliana, whose love has healed me and whose prayers have upheld me during the most challenging times of my life.

A heartfelt gratitude to all the remarkable individuals who shared their stories and expertise to this project. Special appreciation goes to Jeff Deckman, Ilissa Miller, Thomas Eckschmidt, Daniel Shai, Terces Engelhart, Nathan Havey, Alejandro Juan Marcos, Keagan Murphy, Tim Hebert, Chloé Valdary, and Eric Pliner.

I'm immensely thankful to all my beta readers! A heartfelt shoutout to Carol Digan, Michael Trachtman, Tanvir Singh, Brett Anderson, Claudia Neira, Daniel Shai, Erica Dodge, Julien Lafleur, Yamil Y. Baez, and Craig Shoemake for going out of their way to provide honest and invaluable feedback to early pieces of the manuscript.

Also, I'm deeply grateful to my early supporters, who believed in me and contributed financially to my presale campaign. Their support helped me raise $7,261 for the publication of this book.

Your support was a beacon of motivation through the most challenging days. Thank you for your presence in this new chapter of my life.

Dottie Barr
Mayor Jorge Elorza
Milagros Belaunde
Dan Crocker
Brett Anderson
Alfredo Lacayo
Valerie Antonio-Cardozo
Julie Sullivan Owens
Carolina Sanchez
Michael LaRhette
Gerry A. Fernandez
John Pagliarini
Al Cumplido
Carol Digan
Sandra McNamara
Lorne Adrain
Luma Samara
Antonio Zafra
Jeshua Zapata
Dr. Candida Castillo
Tomas Avila
Oscar Lozano
Luann Edwards
Bethany Warburton
Gisella Soriano
Rick Wessels
Karen King
Eric Koester

Agnieszka Raczynska
Arlene Coffman
Josh Steinberg
Daniel E. Jennings
Kara Lund
Brian Hull
Cecil Cox
Julie Meyers
Heidi Kranz
Ines Echevarria
Alejandro Tirado, PhD
Erica Dodge
Aurora Paul
Jo Self
Jenifer Giroux
Allison Sherman
Timothy Sullivan, MBA
Paula Delmenico
Rick Anderson
Julia McDowell
Norelys Consuegra
Leonard Aaron Caplan
Kyle Bennett
Jeremiah Poage
Art Fromm
Kathy Bendheim
Jocelyn Tuttle
Keri Ambrosino
Vanessa Toledo
Ron Crosson
Randall Sacilotto
Katherine Batson

Yamil Y. Baez

Joshua Lavoie

Elizabeth M. Tanner, Esq.

Anthony Botelho

Rodrigo Tempestini

Melida Anyi Espinal

Maria Guevara

Bethany Hashway

Claudia Neira

Joan Munoz

I deeply appreciate the support I've received from each of you, as well as from many others. Your belief in this project means the world to me. Thank you.

# Recommended Reading

---

Below are books that have deeply impacted my worldview and directed my current path. My goal is to offer you new reading recommendations or inspire you to share these insightful works with others who could benefit from them.

**PERSONAL AND SPIRITUAL GROWTH:**
- *The Four Agreements: A Practical Guide to Personal Freedom* by don Miguel Ruiz
- *The Mastery of Self: A Toltec Guide to Personal Freedom* by don Miguel Ruiz Jr.
- *Think Like a Monk: Train Your Mind for Peace and Purpose Every Day* by Jay Shetty
- *The Artist's Way: A Spiritual Path to Higher Creativity* by Julia Cameron
- *Atlas of the Heart: Mapping Meaningful Connection and the Language of Human Experience* by Brené Brown
- *Braving the Wilderness: The Quest for True Belonging and the Courage to Stand Alone* by Brené Brown
- *The Body Keeps the Score: Brain, Mind, and Body in the Healing of Trauma* by Bessel van der Kolk, MD

- *The Power of Intention: Learning to Co-create Your World Your Way* by Wayne W. Dyer
- *The Seven Spiritual Laws of Success: A Practical Guide to the Fulfillment of Your Dreams* by Deepak Chopra
- *Living in the Light: Yoga for Self-Realization* by Deepak Chopra and Sarah Platt-Finger
- *All for Love: The Transformative Power of Holding Space* by Matt Kahn
- *The Untethered Soul: The Journey Beyond Yourself* by Michael A. Singer
- *The Alchemist: A Fable About Following Your Dream* by Paulo Coelho
- *The Essential Rumi* by Coleman Barks
- *The Prophet* by Kahlil Gibran

**LEADERSHIP AND WORKPLACE CULTURE:**

- *Blind Spot: The Global Rise of Unhappiness and How Leaders Missed It* by Jon Clifton
- *Flourish: A Visionary New Understanding of Happiness and Well-Being* by Martin Seligman
- *The Healing Organization: Awakening the Conscience of Business to Help Save the World* by Raj Sisodia and Michael J. Gelb
- *Sacred Commerce: Business as a Path of Awakening* by Matthew Engelhart and Terces Engelhart
- *Conscious Capitalism Field Guide: Tools for Transforming Your Organization* by Raj Sisodia, Timothy Henry, Thomas Eckschmidt, Jessica Agneessens, and Haley Rushing
- *Wellbeing at Work: How to Build Resilient and Thriving Teams* by Jim Clifton and Jim Harter
- *It's the Manager: Moving From Boss to Coach* by Jim Clifton and Jim Harter

- *Culture Shock: An Unstoppable Force is Changing How We Work and Live. Gallup's Solution to the Biggest Leadership Issue of Our Time* by Jim Clifton and Jim Harter
- *Love Leadership: The New Way to Lead in a Fear-Based World* by John Hope Bryant
- *Love + Work: How to Find What You Love, Love What You Do, and Do It for the Rest of Your Life* by Marcus Buckingham
- *Search Inside Yourself: The Unexpected Path to Achieving Success, Happiness (and World Peace)* by Chade-Meng Tan
- *The Tao of Leadership: Lao Tzu's Tao Te Ching Adapted for a New Age* by John Heider

# Appendix

—

**Introduction**

1. Brown, Brené. 2010. *The Gifts of Imperfection: Let Go of Who You Think You're Supposed to Be and Embrace Who You Are*. Center City, Minnesota: Hazelden. PDF. https://ia801406.us.archive.org/0/items/the-gifts-of-imperfection/The%20Gifts%20of%20Imperfection.pdf.
2. Clifton, Jon. 2022. *Blind Spot: The Global Rise of Unhappiness and How Leaders Missed It*. Washington, District of Columbia: Gallup Press.
3. Gallup, Inc. 2023. *State of the Global Workplace: 2023 Report*. Omaha, Nebraska: Gallup, Inc.

**Chapter 2—The Struggle Is the Gift**

1. Centers for Disease Control and Prevention. 2021. "Adverse Childhood Experiences (ACEs) Preventing Early Trauma to Improve Adult Health." *VitalSigns* (blog), US Department of Health and Human Services. August 23, 2021. https://www.cdc.gov/vitalsigns/aces/index.html.

2. Hill, Diana. 2023. "What Are the Benefits of Compassion?" *Psychology Today* (blog), *Psychology Today*. April 10, 2023. https://www.psychologytoday.com/us/blog/from-striving-to-thriving/202304/what-are-the-benefits-of-compassion.

**Chapter 4—Transformational Trips: A Journey to Self**

1. Davidson, Katey. 2023. "What Are the Ayurveda Doshas? Vata, Kapha, and Pitta Explained." *Healthline (blog),* Healthline Media. September 19, 2023. https://www.healthline.com/nutrition/vata-dosha-pitta-dosha-kapha-dosha.
2. Kubala, Jillian. 2022. "What Is Ayahuasca? Experience, Benefits, and Side Effects." *Healthline* (blog), Healthline Media. December 16, 2022. https://www.healthline.com/nutrition/ayahuasca.

**Chapter 5—Evolving Through Relationships**

1. Brady, Adam. 2017. "Honoring the Layers of Life in Your Yoga Practice." *Yoga* (blog), Chopra. January 18, 2017. https://chopra.com/blogs/yoga/honoring-the-layers-of-life-in-your-yoga-practice.
2. Endless Satsang Foundation, Inc. 2024. "About Satsang." *Endless Satsang* (blog), Endless Satsang Foundation, Inc. Accessed February 5, 2024. https://endless-satsang.com/about-satsang.
3. Gabriel, Roger. 2022. "Spiritual Intentions on the Path to Enlightenment." *Meditation* (blog), Chopra. January 21, 2022. https://chopra.com/blogs/meditation/spiritual-intentions-on-the-path-to-enlightenment.

4. Perry, Philip. 2017. "This Buddhist Parable Can Ease Your Suffering During a Crisis." *Culture & Religion* (blog), *Big Think*. June 27, 2017. https://bigthink.com/culture-religion/this-buddhist-parable-can-ease-your-pain-during-a-crisis/.
5. Ruiz Jr., don Miguel. 2016. *The Mastery of Self: A Toltec Guide to Personal Freedom.* San Antonio, TX: Hierophant Publishing.

**Chapter 6—A Journey Toward Acceptance**

1. Gallup, Inc. 2022. *Global Emotions Report 2022.* Omaha, Nebraska: Gallup, Inc.

**Chapter 7—We Need Love in the Workplace**

1. Gallup, Inc. 2023. *State of the Global Workplace: 2023 Report.* Omaha, Nebraska: Gallup, Inc.

**Chapter 8—Leaders Who Left a Mark**

1. Bryant, John Hope. 2009. *Love Leadership: The New Way to Lead in a Fear-Based World.* Read by John Hope Bryant. Los Angeles, California: Gildan Media, LLC. Audible, 04:47:00.

**Chapter 9—Longing to Belong**

1. Brown, Brené. 2017. *Braving the Wilderness: The Quest for True Belonging and the Courage to Stand Alone.* Read by Brené Brown. New York, US: Random House Audio. Audible, 04:12:00.
2. Gallup, Inc. 2024. "How to Create a Strengths-Based Company Culture." *CliftonStrengths* (blog), Gallup, Inc.

Accessed January 30, 2024. https://www.gallup.com/
cliftonstrengths/en/290903/how-to-create-strengths-
based-company-culture.aspx.

**Chapter 10—Mindfulness: A Path to Well-Being**

1. Gallup, Inc. 2020. *Employee Burnout: Causes and Cures Report.* Omaha, Nebraska: Gallup, Inc.
2. Kern, Merilee. 2022. "What Is the True Cost of Work-Related Stress?" *The American Institute of Stress* (blog). April 20, 2022. https://www.stress.org/what-is-the-true-cost-of-work-related-stress.
3. Pendell, Ryan. 2022. "Employee Wellbeing Starts at Work." *Workplace* (blog). July 20, 2022. https://www.gallup.com/workplace/394871/employee-wellbeing-starts-work.aspx.
4. Wigert, Ben, and Sangeeta Agrawal. 2018. "Employee Burnout, Part 1: The 5 Main Causes." *Gallup, Inc* (blog). July 12, 2018. https://www.gallup.com/workplace/237059/employee-burnout-part-main-causes.aspx.

**Chapter 11—The Healing Workplace:
A Pathway to Flourishing People**

1. Chapman, Robert. 2012. "Truly Human Leadership: Bob Chapman at TEDxScottAFB." TEDx Talks. June 20, 2012. 00:22:01. https://www.youtube.com/watch?v=njn-lIEv1LU.
2. Conscious Capitalism, Inc. 2024. "Feature: Why Consciousness Is the Key." *Conscious Capitalism* (blog), Conscious Capitalism, Inc. Accessed March 4, 2024. https://www.consciouscapitalism.org/story/feature-why-consciousness-is-the-key.

3. Engelhart, Matthew, and Terces Engelhart. 2008. *Sacred Commerce: Business as a Path of Awakening.* Berkeley, CA: North Atlantic Books.

4. Mackey, John. 2019. "John Mackey, Whole Foods." Conscious Capitalism, Inc. November 18, 2019. 00:44:47. https://www.youtube.com/watch?v=cyf3DJM4XDo&t=19s.

5. Madeson, Melissa. 2017. "Seligman's PERMA+ Model Explained: A Theory of Wellbeing." *Happiness & SWB* (blog), *Positive Psychology.* February 24, 2017. https://positivepsychology.com/perma-model/#plus.

6. Minor, Dylan, and Jan W. Rivkin. 2016. *Truly Human Leadership at Barry-Wehmiller.* New York, NY: Harvard Business Publishing. PDF. https://store.hbr.org/product/truly-human-leadership-at-barry-wehmiller/717420?sku=717420-PDF-ENG.

7. Pierre, Keda Edwards. 2021. "Why Conscious Businesses Will Lead the Next Paradigm Shifts." *Leadership* (blog), *Forbes.* March 23, 2021. https://www.forbes.com/sites/forbescoachescouncil/2021/03/23/why-conscious-businesses-will-lead-the-next-paradigm-shifts/?sh=57af152a66bc.